OVERCOMING THE SPIRIT OF

POVERTY

Removing Obstacles That block Kingdom Provision

ABRAHAM JOHN

Overcoming the Spirit of Poverty
Removing Obstacles that Block Kingdom Provision

First Edition 2004
Second Edition 2025

Copyright © 2004 Abraham John (First Edition)
Second Edition © 2025 Abraham John

Published by Abraham John
www.TheKingdomNetwork.org
email: info@thekingdomnetwork.org
1(800) 558 5020

ISBN: 978-1-948330-49-7

Contents

Contents

Preface

As soon as some people hear the word "poverty," they immediately think of a specific geographical area. They assume that poverty exists only in developing countries. However, this book is written just for you, no matter your geographical location, social status, color or race.

Everyone born under the sun is equally affected by this spirit in one way or other. I have not yet met a person who is happy and content being poor. No one is exempt. All human beings struggle equally to overcome this spirit.

Jesus became poor, not only to save a few impoverished people. Just as He became sin to redeem all sinners, for your benefit, He became poor so that you, through His poverty, we may become rich:

> *For you know the grace of our Lord Jesus Christ, that though He was rich, yet for your sakes He became poor, that you through His poverty might become rich.*
> 2 Corinthians 8:9

This spirit of poverty does not respect anyone. From the palace to the bustling streets of Calcutta, India, it poses a threat to humanity's very existence. Why is this the case? You may wonder how this could be. You are not poor; you are living a better life than 75% of the world's population. This is precisely why God inspired me to write this particular book.

Any area of your life where you experience lack, scarcity, dissatisfaction, unfruitfulness, unproductiveness, or repeated failures indicates that the spirit of poverty is at work.

As a sequel to "Sin, Flesh & the Devil," this book will only be a blessing to those who have victory over sin, flesh, and the devil. Having a lot of money is not an indication that you are free from the struggles of poverty. The Bible does not equate wealth and prosperity or blessedness necessarily with money and possessions (Luke 12:15).

If the church is to make an impact on this earth, which must happen, it will only succeed when we break the hold of the spirit of poverty on our lives.

Many strong men and women feel trapped due to a lack of resources. They are disappointed and dissatisfied with their lives, and their dreams feel almost dead. But God is merciful, using even a raven or a donkey to fulfill His purpose.

Millions have slipped into eternity without hearing the gospel of the kingdom because the church lacked the resources to evangelize them. Don't we feel any remorse or guilt knowing that thousands of people are going to hell every week in Africa and Asia without Christ? Has our heart become so calloused that we no longer feel the pain and deprivation of others?

This is the second book the Lord gave me to write.

I was fasting and seeking the Lord for breakthroughs in my life. One of the questions I asked Him was, "Lord, You gave me this huge vision and big dreams for Your kingdom, where is the money going to come from?" He said, "money is not the problem. You overcome the spirit of poverty, and money won't be a problem."

One morning when I awoke, I felt like revelation flooding my spirit. I said to myself, that I had better go and start writing it down.

I went to my desk and took up a notebook, and started writing what was coming to my spirit.

I started writing at 6.30am in the morning, and I kept on writing throughout the day. The flow of revelation stopped when it reached 9.30pm. I took what I wrote in my notebook, and I noticed God was answering my questions through what I had written. He said to me, "This is not just for you. There are others who are looking for the same answers."

What you read in this book is what the Lord gave me that day. I believe it will bless you and answer some of the questions you have been struggling with in your life.

I grew up sleeping on a concrete floor for the first eighteen years of my life. Now when I look back, I can see that the Lord took me from where I was, and made me a blessing to the nations of the world. This is the Lord's doing. If He can use me, then He will use anyone.

In this book, we are going to deal with one of the most formidable forces that hinders us from fulfilling what God has called us to do, and which blocks us from experiencing what He has promised—the spirit of poverty. Welcome to the journey.

Introduction

How many are waiting for the wealth of Egypt, the riches of the wicked, to be transferred to them? It won't come unless you break the twisted power of the spirit of poverty from your life. You must prepare your life so that the ultimate wealth transfer can occur for the body of Christ.

Sometimes I wonder why so many ungodly idol-worshipers acquire great wealth and riches while the spirit of poverty seems to have no effect on them. The reason is that they have formed a pact with other demon spirits who granted them that wealth; otherwise, they wouldn't survive even a day.

Whenever a business is established in India, for example, the first thing they do is seek favor by appeasing the spiritual principality or deity that rule that area. They offer sacrifices, food, money, and blood to appease these dark forces in order to invoke their favor.

But we, as the church, remain powerless, although not for long. We aspire to assist the less fortunate, offer shelters for the homeless, establish colleges and universities, and create TV and broadcasting stations; yet our resources remain depleted.

This situation must come to an end once and for all. However, this change will occur only when we receive the revelation from God's Word that is necessary for this generation. Someone must pay the price. We need a Moses, a Nehemiah, or a Joseph. The just shall be delivered through knowledge (Proverbs 11:9b).

Whenever God did something for His kingdom, He consistently utilized the wealth of the wicked. Moses, David, Nehemiah, and Joseph were all entrusted with the wealth of the wicked in order to fulfil their respective destinies. To experience such provision in your life, you must prepare yourself.

MISCONCEPTIONS THAT LIMIT GOD'S PURPOSE

Many believers of God have accepted their poverty as if it came directly from God. Unable to find a way out, they have submitted to it, and now they and their families are suffering because of it. They think poverty is a blessing, believing it will lead to better rewards in heaven.

They don't care about their neighbors going to hell; instead, they focus on remaining poor and worrying about their place in heaven. They don't realize that if they had more resources, they could win a few more souls for Jesus. They are deceived.

The greatest deception the devil ever orchestrated was convincing people that he doesn't exist.

They believe that if we try to do too many things for God, it will cause us to sin. If we undertake something significant for God, it is considered worldly, as only worldly people engage in great endeavors, not the spiritual. If we possess too much money, we won't be spiritual. These are all indicators that the spirit of poverty is at work.

They believe that driving an expensive car leads to pride and detracts from glorifying God. They are unwilling for their children to attend good schools because such schools are viewed as worldly and unchurched.

Have you ever encountered people like this? You can reflect on the rest yourself. Which areas of your life require deliverance from this spirit?

God help us and have mercy upon us. The gospel is not complete if we only share Jesus with the hungry and do not provide them with anything to eat. If we preach healing but are unable to bring relief even for a cold or flu, let alone build a hospital for them, what are we really saying? Or, if we proclaim the love of Jesus to the naked but fail to give them anything to cover their nakedness, what kind of gospel and God are we representing?

How many millions in Africa and India would have come to Christ even ten years ago if the church had been equipped to preach the "full gospel of the Kingdom"? When we observe the world, we feel embarrassed about what they achieve in the areas of business, innovation, media, and more.

The church has maintained her silence because we know that if we raise our voices, we must have the means to act. Enough is enough. Let us come to our senses and recognize who we are and what we have been entrusted to do.

Poverty affects various aspects of life in different ways. It is not limited to finances alone. Satan's plan is to keep us impoverished and suffering in every area of our lives. The devil consistently opposes freedom and growth. He looks for ways to bind people and keep them in bondage

FINANCIAL FREEDOM

Through His teaching on prayer, Jesus conveyed what He desires to see achieved on this earth:

Hallowed be Your Name

The first need was that the Father's Name to be hallowed or glorified. How can we glorify God's name in our lives?

Will we glorify the Father if we live in lack, sickness, or debt, while being unproductive, mediocre, ignorant, and unloving? I don't think so. However, the opposite will bring Him glory. Therefore, our goal in all our endeavors should be to bring glory to His Name.

It is beneficial for us to make an inventory of our lives and ask ourselves: In which areas do we glorify God, and in which we do not? Before you read this book, take a moment to consider whether you are bringing the maximum glory possible to the Lord and His kingdom through your life, your family, your work, and elsewhere.

We bring glory to Him when we make the most of everything He has provided to us. Anything less than our best is unacceptable to God. With our sacrifice or service, are we offering Him our best?

The Bible tells us that whatever we don't maximize will be taken from us and given to someone who will use it for His glory (Matthew 25:28). This is why many in Christian circles go from bad to worse.

If we do not glorify God with our bodies, it will affect our well-being (see 1 Corinthians 6:19). We honor God through our actions with our bodies. He desires our best from our body, our mind, our spirit, our abilities, our talents, and more besides.

His Kingdom Come

The second need was for His kingdom to come to this earth. He is the King of kings, and He wants to see His kingdom established here. While He reigns over all, He has entrusted this task to us. So, what are we doing with it?

We go to church on Sundays to show our attendance. Will this help establish His Kingdom?

Our constant striving and purpose should be to witness His kingdom come upon this earth. Many believe God's kingdom will only come during the millennium. Jesus did not ask us to pray about the Millennium, even though the fullness of His kingdom will only manifest then. At this moment, He desires to see as much of this earth as possible come under His rulership (1 Corinthians 15:25-28).

We have an enemy who dislikes seeing us maximize our lives for God so that His kingdom can be established on earth instead of the kingdom of darkness.

If the spirit of poverty were not at work on this earth, His kingdom would be much larger now.

His Will be Done on Earth

The third need is to see His will done here and now on this earth as it is in heaven. It is God's desire for His will to be fulfilled in our lives just as it is in heaven.

God has a pre-planned will and purpose for our lives. It is our choice whether to follow it. This means that whatever God planned for our lives before the foundation of the world should manifest now.

Unfortunately, most of the church members you know are unaware of their God-given purpose or even God's will for their lives.

The enemy's plan is to steal, kill, and destroy. He aims to steal whatever God has provided us. If many have died before us without fulfilling God's will for their lives, what is the reason for this? Who blinded them so they could not see God's purpose or calling? I believe it was the enemy.

God has a will for every aspect of your life: your work, finances, family, marriage, health, destiny, relationships, and wisdom—almost everything, in fact. His will is for it to be achieved on earth as He has planned in heaven.

Anything that keeps you from fulfilling God's plan for your life is the result of this same spirit at work in your life. It withholds God's resources from you, preventing you from answering God's call, while many people continue to slip into hell because of this ugly demon's diabolic influence.

Whatever makes you miserable and gives your life an illusionary feel, is the work of this devil. He has remained hidden for thousands of years. However, in His mercy, God has revealed it to us in this time so that we can fulfill His purpose on this earth.

How many visions and dreams have perished or remain unfulfilled because people couldn't find the resources to realize them? How many mission trips were canceled and plans to go to colleges set aside due to insufficient funding? How many men and women didn't complete their education because they lacked support? How many talents and abilities remain undeveloped because people found no opportunities to utilize them?

Whatever prevents us from living up to what God desires for us, is the direct work of the spirit of poverty.

One of the major strongholds preventing the church from evangelizing the world today is not necessarily the stronghold of religion or witchcraft, as some may think; rather, it is the stronghold of poverty.

We lack resources, anointing, power, and wisdom. How many ministries could have accomplished far more; and, how many more individuals may have entered the mission field, if the church were willing to cover the costs for them to go and fulfill what God called them to do?

Dear child of God, please open your heart and spirit to receive what the Spirit is saying to the churches. I believe this book will both bless you and revolutionize your life. Your life will never be the same again. After reading this book, you may no longer ask the question, "Why?" again.

CHAPTER 1

The Spirit of Poverty

The spirit of poverty can affect nearly every area of one's life. If you are experiencing a lack of love in your marriage, diminished productivity or inhibited creativity, no favor with God or others, a dry spirit, a deficiency in the fruit of the Spirit and gifts of the Holy Spirit, or a lack of anointing, then it is time to take action.

You may have money, but somehow you can't seem to benefit from it, whether due to a lack of wisdom or poor health. The inability to give and an inability to receive love are some of the symptoms of the work of a spirit of poverty.

God wants His church to be prepared for the looming economic crisis. The only way to safeguard yourself, is to be liberated from the spirit of poverty. Many will find themselves in this crisis if they don't change their mindsets and equip themselves.

Preparing for this is not about investing in the stock market, real estate, or savings. When God transfers wealth, the people who benefit are not necessarily those who are financially savvy. We see repeated examples in the Bible where those who benefited from wealth transfers positioned themselves according to divine destiny. People—like Joseph, the Israelites, the widow in 2 Kings 4, and Nehemiah—were blessed by the wealth of the wicked coming into their lives.

Any wealth you acquire without being released from this bondage will lead you away from God. The devil operates through deception. He may bestow riches upon you, but will leave you lacking in other aspects of your life, as he is not limited to finances alone.

However, the wealth you acquire after being freed from the spirit of poverty will be used for God's kingdom and His glory, bringing others and yourself closer to Him. Jesus referred to this in Luke 12:16-21, where a spirit of poverty influenced a rich man:

Then He spoke a parable to them, saying:

"The ground of a certain rich man yielded plentifully. And he thought within himself, saying, 'What shall I do, since I have no room to store my crops?' So he said, 'I will do this: I will pull down my barns and build greater, and there I will store all my crops and my goods. And I will say to my soul, "Soul, you have many goods laid up for many years; take your ease; eat, drink, and be merry."'

But God said to him, 'Fool! This night your soul will be required of you; then whose will those things be which you have provided?'

"So is he who lays up treasure for himself, and is not rich toward God."

In verse 21, Jesus stated that he is not rich, even though, according to worldly standards, others perceived him as wealthy. To Jesus, the man was poor because he lacked many of the things available to him, such as peace, hope, and eternal life. In God's eyes, he was poor. You need God's report for your life.

Satan has made many people materially wealthy, only to leave them spiritually poor. Similarly, others who are spiritually wealthy remain materially poor. As a child of God, you deserve both types of wealth: spiritual and natural. It is essential to be balanced in both areas in order to realize your dreams and visions for God's kingdom and His glory.

As you insist on freedom from the yoke of the devil, he will only free you in the specific areas that you require. Many are freed in their spirits but suffer in their bodies. Others are free in their bodies, but not in their spirits. Some may be free, yet their families remain in bondage. Perhaps they are struggling in their businesses or in their relationships. Or maybe they never seem to grow in their walk with the Lord.

If riches could corrupt us, they might have already corrupted many of the saints in the Old Testament, from Abraham to David. Most people desire to be materially wealthy when they hear about being freed from the spirit of poverty; however, true wealth and prosperity lie in being able to live happily with or without money in Christ.

Paul lived by this principle. He learned to be content in whatever situation he was in, yet remained happy and fulfilled his calling (Philippians 4:12).

This is what you need. Nothing should stop you from fully committing to God and serving Him. Nothing should hinder you or prevent you from accomplishing God's will; His will must be done on earth as it is in heaven. You need to embrace the kingdom life.

When Jesus is your King, you can do whatever He desires—not based on your bank account or income. If your plans rely on finances, then the spirit of poverty binds you. When you give to the poor, if you typically give the least instead of the best, then the spirit of poverty is at work.

MANIFESTATIONS OF THIS SPIRIT

There are four scriptural indicators of a spirit of poverty oppressing your life.

Hinderance from fulfilling God's purpose (Mark 1:23-26)

You go to church, you sing the songs, and fellowship with the brethren, yet you feel bound and are not doing what God created you to do. You seem merely satisfied with what you have and where you are. This spirit robs you of your purpose in God, making you mediocre and ineffective.

Spirit of confusion and greed

Spirits of confusion and greed support the second aspect, as these keep you selfish. They will bind your hands so that you cannot give to anyone. This was the case with the man who had a withered hand (Mark 3:3-5).

A withered hand is one that cannot extend toward others to bless them; it always remains close to the body. Such a person may possess things, but does not share them. This is a curse, for the Bible declares that when you give, you will receive more.

Preventing you from functioning within God's original design

The third aspect is that this spirit prevents you from functioning as God intended you to function. We see this in the woman who was bound by Satan and bent over for eighteen years, unable to raise herself up (Luke 13:10-13).

Such a person may desire to do many things for God but is hindered by the infirmity of their body. These individuals remain bound by the weight they carry. What brings burdens is the yoke of the devil.

Many are bent over by debt and their past, making it difficult for them to function as God intended. When they wish to contribute more to God and His kingdom, an unexpected bill arrives, taking that money out of their hands. Many are constrained by extra responsibilities. They become involved in too many activities and are ineffective in any of them.

Relying on and depending on others to meet your needs

The fourth aspect is depending on others to meet your needs, instead of trusting God for those things. When you trust God, He often works through other people; however, when you make them your source instead of Him, you fall into another of the enemy's traps and into bondage.

We see this in John chapter five, with the paralyzed man. He didn't have anyone to help him get into the waters of the Pool of Siloam. This left him poor, sick, and destitute for thirty-eight years.

Even though God, Himself, appeared before him, he was still waiting for someone to come along to help him reach the water. Then, when the help that he was waiting for, finally arrived, he was not able to recognize it nor receive it.

Can you recognize if any area of your life is affected by this spirit?

CHAPTER 2

The Entrance of the Spirit of Poverty

Spirits exist independent of a physical body. If they wish to operate on Earth, they require an earthly body or substance. Therefore, they are effectively illegal intruders who work through deception, ignorance, and misrepresentation. For a spirit to gain entry to a location, an earthly family, or an individual, they legally need an opened door.

They use sin, curses, words, imaginations, thoughts, actions, and even objects to weave their way into human lives and communities. In some pagan cultures, this is known as invoking spirits. This occurs when individuals intentionally create a legal entry for demons to operate. It often happens through idol worship, sacrifice, bodily piercings, sexual acts, sin, and any behavior that contradicts God's order of things.

Curses from Adam's disobedience and your father's iniquities offer an entrance for evil spirits. These spirits move from person to person, from nation to nation, and from country to country. They can be transferred through touch, smell, witchcraft, objects, sorcery, enchantments, incantations, chants, mantras and so on.

My purpose here is not to address demonology specifically, but rather to demonstrate how a spirit of poverty enters this world and impacts your life.

Whatever God created was perfect and blessed. The Bible states in Genesis 1:31, "Then God saw everything that He had made, and indeed *it was* very good. So, the evening and the morning were the sixth day."

When God created the earth, it was a perfect place. Everything grew in abundance, and the earth was blessed. You and I know that the opposite of blessing is a curse or poverty. He planted a garden with all the good trees that bore fruit (Genesis 2:9).

Man was placed in a delightful world. There was no shortage of any kind, from food to God's glory, from love to self-esteem, and from health to wisdom. Man lacked nothing. Life on earth was as it is in heaven. God's will prevailed on earth as it does in heaven. His name was glorified, and His kingdom was established, from favor to prosperity, from beauty to zeal.

The enemy observed this and felt envious. He deceived Eve, leading her to disobey God's command. As a result, the power and mystery known as *sin* entered the world, bringing death. Transgression led to sin, and sin brought curse.

Whenever transgression, sin, and curses are in effect, they create a legal dwelling place for evil spirits. Curses provide a legal gateway for demons to operate. Demons do not bring curses; rather, curses invite demons.

Consequently, God pronounced judgment and curses upon the earth. Genesis 3:17-18 says, "Then to Adam He said, "Because you have heeded the voice of your wife, and have eaten from the tree of which I commanded you, saying, 'You shall not eat of it': "Cursed *is* the ground for your sake; In toil, you shall eat of it all the days of your life. Both thorns and thistles it shall bring forth for you, and you shall eat the herb of the field. In the sweat of your face you shall eat bread till you return to the ground, for out of it you were taken; for dust you *are,* And to dust you shall return."

When God spoke that word, 'boom,' the spirit of poverty found a legal avenue to operate on earth. One reason this spirit has remained so strong and powerful over nations for centuries is that it functions under the curse God pronounced over the earth. The very Word of God granted them a legal entry into the atmosphere. Since that day, they have been operating across the face of the earth.

Human beings are the legal and spiritual guardians on this planet. And, because of this, I believe that since the fall of man, every sinful action and word provides an opening and legal entry for its corresponding demon to operate on Earth.

The act of disobedience and the subsequent pronouncement of the curse allowed evil spirits to operate on this earth. The earth was cursed, and it could no longer produce at its full capacity; instead, only thorns and thistles grew naturally.

There are many plants and herbs that you don't want growing in your backyard. The word for thorn in Hebrew is 'kotse,' which means thorn or pricking. The concept of a 'thorn' is often used metaphorically to represent challenges, struggles, or the consequences of sin.

This concept has two further meanings. God told the Israelites that if they didn't destroy their enemies as He commanded, those enemies would become like thorns in their eyes and sides (Joshua 23:13). Here, God uses the term to refer to their enemies. While the Israelites faced natural enemies of flesh and blood, you and I confront spiritual enemies.

Apostle Paul used the same terminology "thorn in the flesh" in his epistles. He alluded to it as a messenger of Satan sent to buffeted him. It could have been an evil spirit from Satan that was tormenting him, not any sickness as many think (Numbers 37:55;

2 Corinthians 12:7). Rather, he was referring to the persecutions he faced by the Judaizers wherever he went.

From Genesis chapter three onward, the earth ceased to yield or provide its best. Men no longer received a harvest that matched their labor. When your land does not produce its fruits, it is a sign of the curse and poverty.

When God led the people of Israel into Canaan, He spoke extensively about their land. He blessed their land, and the spirit of poverty was broken. The curse was lifted. Unless we do the same in our lives, that spirit's effect continues unabated.

Jesus wore a crown of thorns, illustrating that He bore the curse intended for us (Galatians 3:13). He delivered us from that curse of the law by becoming a curse for us.

So, when God said there would be thorns and thistles emerging from the ground, He was referring to both the natural and the spiritual realms. Revelation 9:15 states that there are evil spirits beneath the earth and on the earth.

The spirit of poverty itself has a wide-ranging scope of operation. Similar to the spirit of Jezebel, it ranks among the major *principalities* currently active in the world, impacting upon nearly every area of life.

Its focus is not solely on money. Instead, it seeks to close every door that can bring blessings into your life. It will influence your mind, creativity, vision, purpose, relationships, favor, intelligence, wisdom, knowledge, body, land, education, friendships, influence, and more.

All have fallen short of God's glory. Romans 3:23 states, "For all have sinned and fall short of the glory of God." God's glory is what He originally bestowed upon man, along with His image and likeness. We were created to live in God's glory. To live in God's glory means to live in abundance and safety in every area of our lives.

Anything that causes shortages, lack, and depletion, stems from a spirit of poverty. Everyone has experienced a deficiency of God's glory, and thus, no one is exempt from this spirit's influence and oppression. Every person born on this earth requires some form of deliverance from this evil spirit.

WHY JESUS CAME

Why did Jesus come? Luke 4:18 says, "The spirit of the Lord is upon me, because He has anointed me to preach the gospel to the poor."

Who are the poor mentioned here? Everyone is poor. Even someone who has money can be poor in some areas of their lives. Thus, everyone is poor in this sense of the word. The person who has money may be poor in other areas of life—perhaps in love, relationships, joy, health, or peace.

Jesus came to reach out to everyone affected by the spirit of poverty. The most severe form of poverty is spiritual poverty. You desire to know God, but struggle with your shortcomings. You find it difficult to reach Him through the pressure and clamor of the crowd.

Jesus Became Poor to Make us Rich

Whenever we fall short of God's glory, we cannot become everything He desires for us to be. Every aspect of our lives should reflect God's glory. As Jesus said, "Your will be done, on earth as it is in heaven."

Jesus restored God's glory to us. John 17:22 says, "And the glory which You gave Me I have given them, that they may be one just as We are one:"

What is the glory of a thing or a person? Its glory is when it shines in its maximized state. The glory of the sun is when it radiates with all its strength. The glory of a king is his thriving kingdom. The glory of a person is when he or she fulfills the maximum potential that he or she can achieve.

Whenever a relationship ends, this spirit may gain access. I have observed adopted children encountering this issue. Thus, foster parenting and premarital relationships also serve as gateways for this spirit. Abusive relationships likewise provide entry for this spirit.

The lives of those who remain married but have a relationship that is cold and filled with strife, along with the lives of children who were neglected and do not receive enough love while growing up, also allow for the spirit of poverty to take root.

Wherever there is disunity—whether in the family, church, ministry, or business—the spirit of poverty will be at work.

CHAPTER 3

How the Spirit of Poverty Works

The spirit of poverty operates in every culture and nation across the globe and does not discriminate. It affects both wealthy and poor families, from billion-dollar corporations to the beggar on the street. Whether a person earns six dollars an hour from a disadvantaged background or one who makes 600 dollars an hour from an affluent family—all believers and non-believers, ministers and lawyers, kings and queens are influenced by this spirit, as it keeps them lacking in at least one area of their lives.

Jesus came that we might have life and life more abundantly (John 10:10b).

This is a universal problem, not just a continental one. If we are going to make an impact for God in this generation, we need to seek deliverance from it.

A PRINCIPALITY

The spirit of poverty is a principality, with many other demons operating under its authority. This principality exerts influence over churches, nations, and cultures around the world.

One or more demons under this principality control everything that hinders you from fulfilling God's plan for your life. Anything that makes you dysfunctional in the kingdom of God originates from this principality. Even the spirit of infirmity operates under this master.

Jesus, in His earthly ministry, dealt with the spirit of poverty more than any other. What kept the Israelites in bondage was the spirit of poverty. Jesus addressed giving more than just a few times.

So, He said: "Truly I say to you that this poor widow has put in more than all;" (Luke 21:3). She was liberated from the spirit of poverty. Others were wealthy but didn't contribute because they were bound by that same spirit.

The brother of the prodigal son was also operating under the bondage of the spirit of poverty. Although his father had everything he needed, he never enjoyed any of those blessings. He was more miserable than the servants working for him.

Some of the most powerful words Jesus spoke concerned this son and his relationship with his father. He said, "And he said to him, 'Son, you are always with me, and all that I have is yours." (Luke 15:31). Can you imagine someone is an heir of considerable wealth and are not able to benefit from it and lives like a pauper? This older brother was one such.

Anything that prevents you and me from enjoying our Father's blessings comes from the spirit of poverty. Similarly, anything that keeps us unaware and ignorant of what our Father has for us, is also the work of this same spirit.

CO-HEIRS WITH CHRIST

Romans chapter 8:17 tells us that if we are the children of God then we are co-heirs with Christ:

> And if children, then heirs—heirs of God and joint heirs with Christ, if indeed we suffer with Him, that we may also be glorified together.

We inherit the blessing of Abraham through Jesus Christ. Our Father has abundant resources to fulfill our dreams and His purpose on this earth. He provides us with more than what we need. There is plenty of bread to spare for everyone (Luke 15:17).

Ephesians 1:3 tells us that God has blessed us with "all" spiritual blessings in heavenly places. If this is true, why do many believers settle for merely speaking in tongues? Why are most unable to walk in the fullness of the Holy Spirit and power? Why does the church today lack so much of God's power and resources?

This principality is at work. However, it is time to wake up and show the world, as well as our enemy, who we truly are-strong and courageous (1 Chronicles 19:13).The spirits of lack, scarcity, shortage, infirmity, greed, covetousness, famine, and debt all operate under this principality. God didn't tell the Israelites that He was leading them to a land of lack, but to a land of abundance that flows with milk and honey.

Those who fear the Lord will not lack for any good thing (Psalm 34:10). If you consistently find yourself short of money, food, joy, or peace, you are under the bondage of lack. If you have been pleading to escape from debt for years, it is time to take decisive action against the spirit of poverty, the thief that has been robbing you for far too long

JESUS' FIRST MIRACLE

The first miracle Jesus performed demonstrated to the world the necessity of breaking the power of lack and the spirit of poverty.

The wedding at Cana in Galilee was the setting for this first miracle (John 2:1-11). You can imagine the embarrassment of the host who organized the wedding. The guests were starting to complain and prepare to leave—this was not a good sign at a Jewish wedding. Jesus performed a miracle by turning water into wine.

If you prepare food at home and always fall short of what you need, or when you receive your salary and find you don't have enough to pay your bills, take steps to end this demon's operation in your home, life, and family

THE FIRST MIRACLES

The first miracle Jesus did was meeting the shortage of wine at a wedding feast. You can imagine the stress the hosts felt when they ran out of wine. The spirit of lack and shortage was behind this incident. Jesus stepped in and met that need, miraculously bringing about an abundance of superior quality wine (John 2:1-11).

The first miracle performed by the Apostles after Pentecost also confronted the spirit of poverty.

In Acts 3:1-7, we read the story of a lame man begging for alms at the beautiful gate of the temple. What made this man a beggar? I believe it was the spirit of poverty that robbed him of his destiny and left him lame from his mother's womb. When God healed him, he no longer begged. The spirit of poverty was broken off his life.

Whenever you move in obedience to God's call, the first spirit you will face is the spirit of poverty. When you wish to do anything for the Lord, the first devil that will oppose you is the spirit of poverty. When you consider going to the mission field, you lack funds. What is that? It is the spirit of poverty at work.

When Abram was called by God and started his journey of obedience to a land God was going to show him, the first thing he faced was a famine in that land. He had to go to Egypt in order to survive (Genesis 12:10).

If you need to build a house or a business, purchase a new car, or conduct television outreach, the first obstacle you will encounter is the spirit of poverty—a lack of resources, money, relationships, wisdom, and such like.

The spirit of poverty affects more than just finances. It is an impoverishing force that leads to personal poverty and drains away your natural strength or potential.

How many dreams and visions are shelved because, as soon as someone is ready to act, this demon intervenes and halts their progress? How many callings, like Abraham's, have been diverted and minimized because individuals failed to overcome the spirit of poverty in their lives?

The term *poverty* encompasses poor conditions, lack, insufficiency, and weakness—depleting God's resources in areas such as money, relationships, love, wisdom, anointing, power, authority, understanding, knowledge, favor, family, education, and much more.

This spirit's mission is to prevent you from progressing in knowing the will of God, thus hindering you from fulfilling His purpose for you. Its aim is to divert you from God's best, leading you to settle for less than you deserve.

This spirit compels you to work even harder for less results. You will toil and toil, yet gather nothing. Your harvest will be meager. Its ultimate goal is to kill and destroy you, leaving you disappointed and dissatisfied.

Most of the men of God in the Bible died with hope, smiling, and blessing their children and grandchildren. They knew their time of death because they had fulfilled God's purpose and were prepared to depart. However, poverty can transform both your life and death into a tragedy.

We need to escape this so that we can be in a position to help as many others as we possibly can. Many people struggle in their lives without understanding the reasons behind their struggles. They attend church faithfully, and even give their tithes and offerings.

One of the things this spirit does, is abort your harvest and thus steals your crops. We find in the Book of Judges that when the Israelites sowed, the Midianites came and destroyed their crops and harvest (Judges 6:3-6).

YOUR FIRST MIRACLE

If you have been sowing faithfully, but are not seeing any return, you need to command that evil devil to take his hands off your harvest. Declare that God says He will rebuke the devourer for our sakes (Malachi 3:11).

However, the Word of God states many other things: including that we are healed, yet so many are sick and afflicted; that whom the Son sets free is free indeed, yet many believers are bound and hopeless.

Jesus died to take away the sin of the world. If so, why are people still going to hell today? Have you encountered any sinners lately? I'm sure you have.

Just because something is written in the Word of God doesn't mean it will automatically manifest and become ours. There are conditions attached to many of the promises, and we need to receive the Word of God, accept Jesus Christ as our Lord and Savior, and activate the Word by applying it in our daily lives (Hebrews 4:2-3).

This is where we need to utilize knowledge (Hosea 4:6). If there's one thing you and I lack today, it is knowledge of God and His Word. In truth, we have barely scratched the surface. We had better wake up and open our eyes before the destroyer comes (Nahum 2:1). Watch your fortress!

THE WISE IN HEART SEEKS OUT KNOWLEDGE

Men of understanding increase in knowledge:

> Wise men lay up knowledge...
> Proverbs 10:14

> The heart of him that hath understanding seeketh knowledge...
> Proverbs 15:14

Our God is a God of knowledge (1 Samuel 2:3). From Him comes all knowledge, wisdom, and understanding.

The spirit of ignorance operates under the principality of poverty, for where there is a lack of anything—whether wisdom, money, health, or more—you know who is in control.

The purpose of this spirit is to impact every area of productivity. The spirit of poverty renders us unproductive. When God cursed the earth, it was akin to cursing man, because man was made from the earth, and he exists on this earth. We rely on the earth and its products to sustain our lives.

When God cursed the earth, its productivity was affected. It became barren, and thorns and thistles began to grow instead.

Do you feel overwhelmed by having everything you don't need in your life yet find it difficult to obtain the things you truly need? This is a result of what happened to the earth. While it started producing things we don't need, creating the things we truly need now requires us to both toil, nurture, and protect them.

You don't need to nurture weeds, thorns, or thistles—they grow effortlessly everywhere. Before the curse, everything we needed grew naturally. There was no tilling the ground nor toiling. Life works the same way: developing good habits requires extra time and effort.

CHAPTER 4

The Redeeming Power of the Blood

We are a privileged group of people. As it says in, 1 Peter:2:9

But you are a chosen generation, a royal priesthood, a holy nation, His own special people…

God has chosen you and me to fulfill His purpose. What makes us peculiar, is that God's plan was revealed to us, and we became partners with God in fulfilling His purpose.

In His own *image* and *likeness*, God created humanity. This means that our spirit possesses the same qualities as God does. We were created to know Him, to have fellowship with Him, to live in His presence and glory, and to exercise dominion over all of His creation (Genesis 1:26 and Psalm 8).

He breathed His own Spirit into us, and we became living souls. The Bible says that God is Spirit (John 4:24). If we share the same Spirit as God, it means we can fellowship with Him on His level and do the things He can do.

We are spirit beings, and what makes us spirit, is that we are not limited by time or space. For our spirit to dwell on earth, He formed us a body from the dust. God created the parts in our body that we need to live on this earth. That dust had no life on its own. God didn't create a living being and then breathe His Spirit into it.

Instead, He made a lifeless image from the earth and breathed into its nostrils. Suddenly, that lifeless collection of dust gained life. Therefore, the life within us comes from the Spirit of God. When the Spirit departs, our bodies return to dust as before.

We have nostrils to smell with, eyes to see with, a mouth to eat and speak with, legs to walk with, and a mind to imagine and create with, among other things. Thus, mankind was the glory or crown of God's creation. He was perfect, holy, righteous, and sinless. There was no poverty, sickness, sorrow, or lack of provision in the garden.

In the Garden of Eden, where God placed the man He created, there was no poverty, sickness, sorrow, or need. The man, Adam, possessed boundless wisdom, knowledge, and understanding. Clothed in the glory of the Lord, he had no need for garments.

The entire Earth belonged to him (Psalm 115:16). He was blessed in every aspect. His thoughts were pure, and the atmosphere was clean and the land orderly. He could talk to God anytime he wished. It was a perfect environment, impossible to fully describe.

This man, Adam, didn't know what pain and death were, because he was never meant to experience them. He didn't know what evil was. Everything lived in harmony and peace. There was no hate or anger, and even the animals loved each other.

The first man's name was Adam, and God formed a woman from his rib; she was named Eve. It's worth noting that God didn't create the woman from dust; instead, He took her out of the man.

He didn't breathe into her a second time. The same spirit and life that was in the man entered into the woman. That is why the Bible collectively refers to both men and women as "sons."

John 1:12 states, "But as many as received Him, to them He gave the power to become the sons of God, even to those who believe in His name." The Bible doesn't say "sons and daughters," because men and women share the same spirit. Only their bodies and functions in life differ in some respect.

God told them to eat from all the trees in the garden except for the one in the midst of it.

Satan was envious of the man, his position, and his perfection; and devised plans to destroy his relationship with God. The serpent was more subtle than the other animals, and thus it beguiled Eve into eating the forbidden fruit and giving it to her husband, Adam.

God had said, that the day they ate of it, they would die. On that day, humanity lost their glory, perfection, and relationship with God, allowing sin to enter the world. Romans 5:12 states, "...by one man sin entered into the world, and death by sin..."

Everything fell under a curse: the earth, the serpent, and both man and woman. Decay infiltrated all of creation. God caused Adam and Eve to leave their home in the garden and enter a place that required hard labor and sweat.

In His mercy and love, God didn't abandon humanity in that state, but devised a plan for their redemption. Once they lost the glory of God, they realized they were naked, prompting God to make garments of animal skin for them and clothe them.

God shed the first blood ever, to cover the man and woman He had created. This was a temporary measure to conceal their nakedness and lost glory. He also had a permanent plan to shed

His own blood to robe them in His glory and righteousness as in the beginning.

Thus, humanity severed its relationship with God, and encountered spiritual death, while also facing natural death from that same day subsequently. Adam lived for only 930 years. For God, a thousand years is like one day (1 Peter 3:8; 2 Peter 3:8). It is God's decree that the soul that sins must die, and without the shedding of blood, there is no redemption.

WHAT IS REDEMPTION?

Redemption involves reclaiming what was lost or restoring something to its original owner, ultimately redeeming—buying back what was yours.

We will examine the Israelites' journey in order to understand how God liberated them from bondage in Egypt, which serves as a precursor for the redemption we receive through Christ.

Many see this as an Old Testament story rather than a lesson to teach us the truth. When the Israelites left Egypt, they didn't bind Pharaoh but freed themselves from his grasp. Their struggle did not save them from Egypt; it was God fighting for them through Moses.

When they departed, Egypt remained, and Pharaoh was still alive. Later, as their enemies pursued them, God fought for His people and destroyed their foes.

The devil does not want us to experience freedom in any area of our lives. It resembles Pharaoh's insistence that Moses could lead the Israelites to worship their God but not go too far.

After battling the devil for a time, he will eventually lose ground. Many people stop after they have the "Born Again" experience, while other areas of their lives remain in bondage.

We are spiritual beings living in the natural world, with social, family, and psychological lives. It is important for us to experience and maintain freedom in these and other aspects of life.

A person remains enslaved until they seek liberation. Liberation arises from our intentional desire and demand. The adversary influences individuals to maintain their enslavement and captivity. He opposes relationships based on equality, instead choosing to torment, dominate, and subjugate others.

Jesus' ministry focuses on liberating individuals, helping them to live freely, and subsequently enabling them to assist others in achieving freedom.

In order to explore this further, we will examine the lives of the Israelites and the areas where they found freedom after being released from Egypt. Through this study, I realized that Jesus didn't just die for me to go to heaven, but also for me to experience freedom in every aspect of my life.

FREEDOM IN ALL ASPECTS OF MY LIFE

Now, let's examine the lives of the Israelites and their deliverance from Egypt. On the very first Passover, each family was instructed to take a lamb and slaughter it on the evening of the fourteenth day of the month (Exodus 12:3-13).

They were directed to apply the lamb's blood to their doorposts so that the destroyer would pass over their homes and families. The angel of death passed over them because of the lamb's blood. The blood of the slain lamb brought about their redemption.

Although Moses served as the spokesman for God, protection and deliverance came through obedience to the Word of God and the application of the blood. Pharaoh was troubled, and a great cry arose throughout all of Egypt as never before. He finally released God's people from their slavery.

God then instructed the Israelites to borrow precious clothing, jewels, gold, and silver from the Egyptians. While this was a spiritual deliverance, we are going to see what else they received, as a result.

With the redemption of their souls, or lives, from Egypt, ten things were restored to them. Something powerful happened to each of them as they sat under the covering of the blood. We will examine each significant area of their lives that was restored by redemption.

1. God's Promise to their Father Abraham

The children of Israel were in bondage for 430 years, living without any sense of promise or hope for their lives.

The promise made to Abraham was restored to them. Similarly, when we experience redemption, our hope and promise are also renewed. We regain our sonship and become part of the family of God. Here's how it happened.

When we believe in Christ, we become a child of God and an heir to the promise God made to Abraham. Most Christians do not understand or comprehend the significance of this Abrahamic Covenant. They believe and act like they are second-class citizens. This is because of the lack of the true understanding of God's Word, and stemming from an orphan spirit and heart.

This means, once you are in Christ, there is no difference between the natural children of Abraham and the spiritual children. We are the spiritual children, adopted or grafted into the same promise. They both have equal access and rights to the promise. There is no difference.

For you are all sons of God through faith in Christ Jesus. For as many of you as were baptized into Christ have put on Christ.

There is neither Jew nor Greek, there is neither slave nor free, there is neither male nor female; for you are all one in Christ Jesus.

And if you are Christ's, then you are Abraham's seed, and heirs according to the promise. Galatians 3:26-29

2. Their Heritage—the Land

The Israelites found themselves enslaved in Egypt without any property. Slaves do not possess anything. When they were redeemed, their right to own land was restored. They transitioned from being slaves to being property and landowners. This is the essence of God's plan.

When the blood of Jesus redeems us, we receive ownership of the earth. Jesus said, "All authority in heaven and on earth has been given to me." We are designed to inherit. Every child of God has an inheritance in Christ, both on this earth and in heaven (Psalm 37). The earth belongs to the children of God, not to the devil (Psalm 115:16; Matthew 5:5). We are here to take possession of the land.

Power in the Blood of Jesus

Just as the blood of the lamb redeemed the Israelites, the blood of the Lamb of God redeems us. To redeem means to buy back or regain ownership. There is power in the blood of Jesus.

The devil stole us, and God bought us back, by paying the highest price—the blood of His only begotten Son. Once someone takes what belongs to you, they must pay the price you demand, in order to reclaim your valuable goods.

We were and are precious in God's sight. He was willing to pay with His best. When we were redeemed, we received a greater redemption than the Israelites because of the blood of Jesus. He died for the remission of the sins of the whole world. We received a better hope and a closer relationship with God than they did:

> But now He has obtained a more excellent ministry, inasmuch as He is also Mediator of a better covenant, which was established on better promises. Hebrews 8:6

3. Their Good Health

These people were in bondage for over 430 years, and I'm sure their health suffered. They didn't receive adequate food to nourish their children. Their bodies may have been weak and emaciated from enduring the scorching summer sun of Egypt outdoors. They were abused, beaten, and tormented.

However, on the night of their redemption, something incredible happened to their bodies. The Bible states that they came out prepared for war (Exodus 13:18). There were no feeble or sick among them (Psalm 105:37). Their bodies, though tortured through slavery, were restored, renewed, and made whole. Everyone was completely healed.

This was perhaps the greatest healing miracle of all time. Over six million people were touched and made whole in one night. Nevertheless, it didn't end there.

When they left Egypt, they not only received their immediate healing, but God made a covenant with them regarding healing. He promised not to bring any of the sicknesses of the Egypt upon them. The first covenant God made with them when they came out of Egypt was a covenant of healing (Exodus 15:28).

Under the Coven ant of Grace

How much more should we embrace the covenant of grace, being redeemed by the blood of Jesus? His ministry on this earth demonstrated that God desires us all to be completely healed: spirit, soul, and body. His sacrifice on the cross achieved this for us. By His stripes, we are healed (1 Peter 2:24).

He wants our bodies to be healthy and strong, so that we can better fulfill His will for us. Sickness does not glorify Him; it brings reproach to His name as it undermines His work on the cross.

If He didn't desire the saints of the Old Testament to suffer from sickness, how much more does He not want His New Testament saints suffering, who are under the better covenant?

You may think about Job, who was afflicted in his body by sickness allowed by Satan—done with God's permission. Although Job was a contemporary of Abraham, he was not part of the covenant of healing.

The church needs to let go of her excuses, and emerge from the bondage of Egypt, in order to enter into the covenant that includes both healing and wholeness in Jesus' name.

Your spirit is the candle of the Lord. If your spirit is healthy and whole, then your entire body will be also. If there is darkness in your spirit, your body likewise will be filled with darkness.

Your outer-life is merely a reflection of your inner-life. Your outer-life should bring glory and honor to your Father in heaven, rather than be a cause of reproach. Therefore, be free in Jesus' name!

4. Their Wealth-Money

The Israelites never received a paycheck for their years of forced labor. When God redeemed them that very night, their wages were paid in full—God transferred the wealth of Egypt to the Israelites.

They received more wealth and riches than they could have accumulated through work and overtime. They used that money and gold throughout their wilderness journey, both for building the tabernacle and later for constructing the temple.

They left Egypt wealthy, not poor. They were impoverished while under the bondage of slavery, but upon their redemption, the spirit of poverty was broken off their lives. They possessed the best of everything Egypt had to offer.

We claim to be redeemed, yet most do not have enough to support their own families, let alone to build the kingdom of God or support ministries. However, the Bible tells us that the wealth of the wicked is stored up for the righteous (Proverbs 13:22). Jesus became poor to free us from the spirit of poverty and to enrich us (John 10:10; Psalm 1:3-4, 34:10; and 2 Corinthians 8:9).

Today, the world wants nothing to do with the church because we fail to practice what we preach. We are unable to deliver what we advertise. Because we don't put our words into action, they perceive us as hypocrites and lazy individuals.

This must change, and it will only occur through those who will break free from the spirit of poverty and its curses.

You may want to argue that Jesus was not wealthy. On the contrary, He never borrowed. He had everything He needed in abundance. He was responsible for taking care of twelve disciples, providing daily food, transportation, and accommodation—without using credit. The Bible notes that Judas was the treasurer (John 13:29). We must cast aside our excuses, and allow the Lord to open our eyes of understanding.

Not only wealth, but when the Israelites reached the Promised Land, it exceeded their expectations. They possessed houses they hadn't built, fields they hadn't cultivated, and vineyards they didn't have to plant—a land flowing with milk and honey (Deuteronomy 6:11).

5. Their Glory

Mankind lost this glory through the fall of Adam in the Garden of Eden. After crossing the Red Sea, a symbol of baptism and leaving the past behind, their fame spread throughout the lands of the region. Kings heard and trembled in fear, and their enemies melted with terror.

God appointed the cloud by day and the pillar of fire by night to guide and protect them. The glory surrounded them day and night (Exodus 13:21-22). God restored their glory as a nation and as His chosen people.

When Jesus arrived, this glory was returned to God's children. Thus, we are a chosen people, a royal priesthood (1 Peter 2:9).

In John 17:22, Jesus says that our glory is restored back to us. He said if our spirit is whole and good, then our entire body will also be whole. If there is darkness in our spirit, our body will be filled with darkness as well. Your external life is simply a reflection of your internal life. Your external life should bring glory and honor to your Father in heaven, rather than serve as a reproach. Therefore, embrace freedom in Jesus' Name!

6. Protection

Back in Egypt, the Israelites were vulnerable to every attack from the enemy. Their taskmasters did as they pleased. Their lives held little or no value. They were whipped and scourged, suffering from sickness and affliction, tortured and abused. They couldn't utter a word against their masters or question them at all. After their redemption, their situation changed completely.

The Pharaoh and his army had pursued them, believing these were merely their old slaves. As they drew closer, they realized it was different. Now, the Lord had become the protector of the Israelites. This began even before their deliverance occurred. When the Lord sent the plagues to Egypt, these did not affect the Israelites. Once they were redeemed, the Lord provided clouds by day and fire by night. They experienced an air-conditioned wilderness.

It's difficult to imagine, because this protection even extended to their shoes and clothing (Deuteronomy 8:4). It was like a divine freezer, but the temperature was comfortable for living.

The Bible states in Psalm 105:14-15:

> He permitted no one to do them wrong; Yes, He rebuked kings for their sakes, saying, "Do not touch My anointed ones, and do My prophets no harm."

No nation could stand against them. The Bible states that those who touched them were touching God's eyes. Just as eagles cover their young with their wings, the Lord covers His people with His wings.

When it comes to us, we have a better covenant. Jesus said, "I give you power over all the power of the enemy, and nothing shall by any means hurt you" (Luke 10:19). Both promises apply to our lives. The blessings of Abraham and Christ's blessings are upon us.

We have the armor of God to withstand all the schemes of the enemy. Jesus also stated that He would be with us even to the end of the age. He will never leave us nor forsake us. Psalm 91 alone, is sufficient to keep us safe until eternity.

7. Provision

In Egypt, they ate what was provided to them. They had no choice of food. In Egypt, they received onions, garlic, cucumbers, and more. After their redemption, they were given food from heaven.

These are the food of angels (Psalm 78:25). It was like an angelic catering service. I believe the food from heaven kept them from natural deterioration. They drank water from the rock (Psalm 105:41). They consumed meat and were nearly destroyed by their murmuring and gluttony. They never had to worry about the next day, because the food came to them every morning.

The food and the cloud protected them from all the natural elements. The Bible says, "The sun shall not smite thee by day, nor the moon by night" (Psalm 121:6).

Jesus told us not to worry about tomorrow but to be content today. He said that if His father feeds the birds and clothes the lilies, how much more would He care for us, since we are even more precious than they are? (Matthew 6:26).

There was no miraculous provision while they were in Egypt, as they were not building God's kingdom. Once they left Egypt, they became God's property. He became their Provider and Protector, because now they are on their way to build God's kingdom or fulfilling His assignment for them.

When we adhere to the principles of the kingdom of God, we are supposed to be free from the cares of the world.

8. Victory Over the Enemy

Redemption is accomplished not by just buying back from the enemy, but after the purchase, God destroyed their enemies.

> ... For the Egyptians whom you see today, you shall see again no more forever. Exodus 14:13

> The LORD is a man of war; the LORD is His name. Exodus 15:3

> He said that He would go before them and fight for them to defeat all their enemies (Deuteronomy 1:30). When they completely obeyed His voice, not a single life was lost among them.

> Jesus did the same for us. He not only paid the price, but also defeated the principalities and powers, taking away their authority (Colossians 2:15). He destroyed the power of sin.

> We have complete and absolute power over the enemy in His name.

9. Victory Over Death

When the angel of death visited Egypt, he didn't touch the lives of the Israelites because they were under the blood. They passed from death to life. Egypt was under the fear of death, but the people of Israel had gladness and joy. The blood preserved their lives.

> When Jesus was raised from the dead, we were raised with Him, and are seated with Him in heavenly places (Ephesians 2:6). Death has no more power over us. We have passed through judgment and inherited eternal life through Jesus Christ.

10. Rest

They inherited the Promised Land known as Canaan. We inherit not only while we are here on earth, but also a heavenly inheritance.

Although they received the land of Canaan, the Bible says they died without entering His rest (Hebrews 3:18 & 19) because they were not made perfect without us (Hebrews 11:40).

They earnestly anticipated a city not made by hands, whose Maker is God (Hebrews 11:10). They looked forward to the days of Christ, the days we are currently living in. It is unfortunate that some wish to return to what the Old Testament saints had, who meanwhile looked forward to what we now possess (Hebrews 3:13-19, 4:1-3).

Some believe we will enter our Canaan only after we die. The Israelites had to conquer their enemies to inherit their Canaan.

Will there be anyone for us to conquer after we die? Many don't want to strive for greatness in the Lord. They prefer a mediocre and unfulfilled life. There is no enemy for us in heaven. Our adversary is here, but has already been defeated by Christ on the cross.

We need to walk by faith as if everything necessary for our lives is complete, because as Jesus said, "It is finished."

CHAPTER 5

Understanding God's Favor

Why do I write about God's favor in a book that addresses the spirit of poverty? It is not enough to be liberated from the spirit of poverty. We need to understand and experience God's favor in our lives in order to fulfill our purposes.

Money alone will not transform us into mighty men and women of God. Money is merely a means, not the source. A person can possess all the money in the world, but it means nothing to them.

Who is your favorite character in the Bible, and why? We all have our favorites, each chosen for different reasons. Perhaps you admire them for their accomplishments in life. It may be their bravery, loving favor, riches, anointing, wisdom, or the miracles they performed. You may believe these individuals possessed unique talents that set them apart from others. However, if you were to take a closer look at their lives, you'll find they were not as "special" as you might think.

They may have been quite ordinary in terms of their human nature. In the letter from James, we learn that the great prophet Elijah was a man with the same passions as you and I:

> Elijah was a man with a nature like ours, and he prayed earnestly that it would not rain; and it did not rain on the land for three years and six months. James 5:17

That means, he used to think about himself as you and I do sometimes. He had the same battles in his mind that he needed to overcome, as you and I do.

One thing is certain though, they all had God's favor on their lives. There was something about their lives that drew God's attention. God delighted in them enough to grant them such favor.

If you and I can learn those secrets from their lives, we too can receive the same blessings. I want to express that God has favorite people. However, the good news is, that anyone can become His favorite. While it's true that God has favorites, He doesn't show partiality.

What does it mean when the Bible says that *your leaves shall not wither?* What kinds of leaves do people like you and I have?

For a tree, the leaves are as important as its roots. The trees cannot live by roots alone. It is through the leaves that it absorbs the sunlight to prepare its food. It is through the leaves that the flower, and then the fruit or seed comes.

I believe that when the Bible refers to our *leaves,* it is saying that our source of income, productivity, and posterity shall not run out when we are planted by the riverside, which is the Spirit of God.

He will always bring us the income we need. He will sustain our lives even by sending ravens. That is how you know whether you have God's favor in your life. It is when you prosper in everything you do, by trusting in Him.

God's favor is a powerful or supernatural ability that He grants to a person to protect, empower, and inform them of things that are naturally impossible. It consistently flows through relationships, covenants, commitments, agreements, partnerships, friendships, family, and much more.

When any of these relationships are dysfunctional it hinders the flow of God's favor from entering into your life. It is akin to a person with bad credit. When he or she tries to buy a car or a house, they do not receive what they desire because lenders will not approve the loan. Why? Their record indicates broken agreements.

It is the same when God wishes to bless someone, but observes broken relationships, covenants, commitments, agreements, partnerships, friendships, and so forth. He withholds His blessings until the matter has been resolved with the other party.

God is love, and we are created in His image and likeness. Therefore, He expects us to walk in love and operate from a place of love. Psalm 133:1 and 3 state, "Behold, how good and how pleasant it is for brethren to dwell together in unity...for there the LORD commanded the blessing, even life forevermore."

WHAT GOD'S FAVOR WILL DO

There are at least four things that God's favor will do for you:

It will protect you

God's favor will safeguard your purpose. It will shield you from your enemies, and keep you focused on your mission.

God will prepare a table before you in the presence of your enemies (Psalm 23:5). This means, your enemies can see you being blessed, but cannot touch you. It will protect your health.

Nothing will harm you; no one can stand against you. You can become an unbeatable one-man army that will astonish the world. God will go ahead of you and vanquish your enemies. His goodness and mercy shall follow you. He will make all the crooked paths straight for you. If God opens a door for you, no one can shut it (Revelation 3:7-8).

God's Favor Will Empower You

You do not rely on your own strength. You cannot fulfill God's purpose for your life through your own abilities, so you need His supernatural power upon you (Psalm 18:29). God's strength becomes yours. When you have God's favor, what He possesses, becomes yours. His resources will be at your service.

You will be able to do things that you once thought would be impossible. God will empower your spirit, soul, and body. You will be transformed from an ordinary person to an extraordinary person.

You won't be guided by your own human capability, but by divine ability. You may be too weak to pray or do anything in your own capacity. God's grace will equip you and empower you to do the things you need to be doing. This is why Paul said in 2 Corinthians 12:9, "His grace is sufficient for me, for when I am weak, then I am strong." God's favor will allow you to do the impossible.

It will Promote You

God's favor will take you places you can't naturally reach. Favor will grant you supernatural access to extraordinary blessings. God's favor will elevate you from the dungeon to the palace. It will position you before kings. Now your head will be lifted above your enemies.

You might not be the qualified individual; you may not be the one who seems intelligent; you may feel invisible, and you might see yourself as a nobody; but God's favor will lift you out of the crowd and from the wilderness, anointing your head with oil.

Those who do not know you will listen to you and obey you because of God's favor:

> Thus says the Lord, The Redeemer of Israel, their Holy One, To Him whom man despises, To Him whom the nation abhors, To the Servant of rulers:

> "Kings shall see and arise, Princes also shall worship, Because of the Lord who is faithful, The Holy One of Israel; And He has chosen You." Isaiah 49:7

God's Favor will Inform You

As the Bible states, the fear of the Lord is the beginning of wisdom. God's favor instills a hunger to learn and understand. It fuels a passion for seeking wisdom and the principles that govern life.

Many people misunderstand this scripture, thinking that simply fearing God is enough, while neglecting to learn. That is not the intention. Rather, it marks the beginning of a journey where wisdom is acquired by any means necessary.

Proverbs 17:16 asks, "Why is there a price in the hand of a fool to obtain wisdom, seeing he has no heart for it?"

Additionally, God's favor provides supernatural knowledge on how to navigate difficult situations. Jesus advised that when you stand before a court, do not worry about how or what you shall answer.

David expressed in Psalm 119:98-99 that God's word makes him wiser than his teachers and enemies:

> *You, through Your commandments, make me wiser*
> *than my enemies;*

*For they are ever with me. I have more under-
standing than all my teachers, for Your testimonies are my meditation.*

Proverbs 2:6 says, "For the Lord gives wisdom; from His
mouth *come* knowledge and understanding;"

Many of us have great dreams to accomplish extraordinary things
for God. It is valuable to study the lives of people whom He used.
They were written not only for preaching but also as examples for
us. If we do what they did, we will achieve the same results.

I was curious about why God chose certain individuals. He
selected one person from a family of twelve or six children and
rejected the others. Often, He chose the person that others deemed
the least likely to succeed. This can lead us to think that God is
partial and loves some more than others.

He accepted Abel and rejected Cain. He chose Noah among
Lamech's many sons and daughters. Terah had three sons: Haran,
Abram, and Nahor. He chose Abram. He selected Jacob and rejected
Esau. He chose Joshua from six million people to be Moses' succes-
sor. David had sixteen sons, but God's choice was Solomon. Jesus
appointed only twelve as His disciples from all those who followed
Him; and the same story continues.

The Bible says in Romans 2:11: "For there is no partiality with God."

Ruth became a great-grandmother of Jesus, even though she was
a Moabite, about whom God said that even the tenth generation shall
not enter the house of God (Deuteronomy 23:3; Nehemiah 13:1).

When I studied the lives of those whom God used to accomplish
His purpose on this earth, I found one thing in common among
them that attracted God's favor.

It was not their education or family background. It was not their abilities or talents. You may have the right education and know the right people, but you may still not be achieving anything with your life. You might have one of the greatest voices for singing and the right vocabulary for every situation. No, no. That is not what God is looking for in your life. These are all secondary to God. When He calls for an interview, He is not asking for your educational resume; He will examine your heart.

It was people's character which captured God's attention. It was their heart. It was their lifestyle that set them apart from others in their family. When God looks at a person, He is not looking for talent; He is looking for character that can be developed.

The Bible states in Proverbs 4:7 that "Wisdom *is* the principal thing; *therefore*, get wisdom. And in all your getting, get understanding."

God works according to principles. So, if you and I learn those principles, we can be used by God. This is what I want to share with you in this book. For indeed, God's eyes are roaming to and fro over all the earth to find those whom He might use (2 Chronicles 16:9).

You may be experiencing struggles in your life. You may have prayed every prayer you can think of, and still received no answer from God. You may have attended every spiritual renewal conference, and still feel as though God is a thousand miles away.

I tell you that many of the answers you seek to your prayers were mentioned in the Bible centuries ago. Many do not read the Bible in order to understand God's revealed will. Instead, they look for a word from a popular TV evangelist. However, they can't believe in the God of the Bible.

I have heard people share the prophetic words they received from various individuals. However, I've heard very few say that

God spoke to them through the Bible. We are becoming a society of Christian celebrities more than Bible-oriented believers.

Many believers are in turmoil because they don't read and study the revealed will of God. How will God reveal the unknown to you when you don't care about or obey His known will? Most believers think they understand the Bible because they hear a twenty-minute sermon each Sunday.

The Bible says in Psalm 119:105 that, "Thy word is a lamp unto my feet and a light unto my path." We use a lamp to see our immediate surroundings and a light to navigate what lies ahead. Everything you need to know to be successful is written in the Word of God. He instructed Joshua to meditate on the Word day and night in order to achieve success wherever he went.

For a fulfilling marriage, principles set by God in the Bible exist.

To achieve financial prosperity, principles are laid out for us in the Word.

Everyone desires success, but few know what it takes or what God's requirements are for achieving it. Everyone wants God's favor, but few understand how to bring God's favor into their lives.

The Bible states in Proverbs 12:2: "A good man obtains favor from the Lord." Additionally, Proverbs 13:15 says: "Good understanding gains favor." From the scripture above, favor is obtainable.

If Ruth and others in the Bible obtained favor from God, I am confident that you and I can achieve it even more. Many people perish for lack of knowledge.

If we have God's favor, we will thrive in all areas of our lives. Our geographical location in this world does not determine our prosperity. The Bible notes that Joseph was prosperous even while in prison.

Have you heard of anyone recently prospering while incarcerated? If God is indeed in the business of granting favor, then why haven't you heard lately of someone flourishing while in prison?

Here's something to consider—if God is in the business of granting favor, why have so many not experienced it?

God wants to see whether you have the character to handle His favor. You need to earn His favor by proving yourself to Him. When God looks at you and me, what He seeks is our character.

Similarly, the devil also targets your character, because he knows that if he can compromise it, you won't achieve God's purpose for your life. If your character doesn't align with your vision, the chances of fulfilling that vision are slim. Your character serves as the foundation upon which your vision is built. Your ministry will never rise above the level of your character.

To me, character means discipline and self-control. It means you are determined to do what you need to do, regardless of the circumstances around you.

If your character is more important to God than your vision, you'll need to learn some principles from the life of someone in the Old Testament who seemed least likely to accomplish anything remarkable. That person is Ruth.

What was so special about her that captivated God to the point of overriding the very law He gave through Moses? Why was she welcomed into God's family when the Scriptures stated that even the tenth generation of Moabites could not enter the house of God?

We are going to examine her life closely to uncover those secrets, so we can gain God's favor and accomplish the vision He has given us.

CHAPTER 6

Principles for Divine Favor

Naomi had two daughters-in-law, Orpah and Ruth. In Ruth 1:10, it is written that both of them expressed a desire to go to Bethlehem with their mother-in-law. And they said to her, "Surely we will return with you to your people."

Orpah reconsidered when she learned about the challenges she would face in Bethlehem. She viewed everything through her own perspective. She realized she wouldn't find a husband, and besides, spiritually 'superior' people would label her an outcast and hurl insults at her. Loneliness, together with no one to confide in as a friend, caused her to withdraw.

Many people are like this. They may be excited about their lives and new projects, but when the slightest problem arises, they quit. They want life to run in cruise control all the time. They dislike change or slowing down for sharp turns. Let me tell you, life is not for quitters.

The Bible says Ruth stuck with her mother-in-law. "Then they lifted up their voices and wept again; and Orpah kissed her mother-in-law, but Ruth clung to her." Ruth 1:14

She made a life-or-death decision. She understood the importance of relationships. She was determined that, no matter what happened, she would stick with her family. She realized that if she distanced herself from her mother-in-law, she wouldn't be able to thrive.

Prosperity comes from favor, and favor stems from relationships. She had a different perspective than Orpah.

Orpah resembled the ten spies who entered the Promised Land. While, Ruth possessed an inquisitive spirit, willing to try something new. She not only wanted to explore new opportunities but was also committed to seeing them through. She didn't say, "I'm going to give it a try for a while. If it doesn't work out for me, I'll return to Moab."

Many fail because they don't attempt anything new. Others fail because they give up when things become challenging. They continue engaging in the same old routines year after year, even though they realize the situation they're in is deteriorating.

Many resemble the impotent man by the pool of Bethesda. He had countless excuses for not being healed but was unwilling to take any action on his own. He waited thirty-eight years for someone to come and assist him. He was so bound to his circumstances that he believed he could never rise above them. Jesus expected a proactive response from him. Unless that man was willing to take some action, even Jesus could do very little for him (John 5:5-6).

Ruth didn't tell herself, "Well, I failed in Moab, so I might fail again. It doesn't matter where I go." She refused to be trapped by the cage of her past experiences. She shattered every boundary and limitation that circumstances tried to impose on her life.

In those days and in her culture, wives were blamed for their husbands' deaths. She was suspected of having been unfaithful, but she didn't let those voices stop her from moving forward with her life. She didn't tell herself, "Now I am worthless. I am not going to try anything new. I will just stay home as a widow, wash dishes, and fold laundry."

God told me recently, that I want to get ahead in life, I need to learn how to handle two things: failures and losses. If I don't approach these two experiences with wisdom, I won't get much further with my dreams.

Setbacks and reroutes are essential on the path to success. This is why I am still not where I want to be in life; I am still in the training camp.

You may think that just because I am writing this, I have achieved everything in life. No. I am on my way though, and I just want to be a blessing to those who are traveling alongside me on the same road. So, if my experience can encourage someone, help them advance, or motivate them to start their own journey, that's what I aspire to do with these books.

If you base your life on desires, they will come and go. You might be waiting for the perfect situation, but even after many years, you could still find yourself stuck in the desire stage.

STAGES FOR FULFILLING YOUR VISION

There are three stages to fulfilling your vision—desire, determination, and discipline.

Desire

God communicates His purpose through our desires. He put an indelible desire in your heart that just won't go away no matter where you are in life.

What you gain, what you lose, and wherever you work, that desire will chase you down like your own shadow. You can't outrun it.

I remember when I was a boy; whenever I got a pen, I used to write the word *desire* in my home language many times. There is nothing more powerful than a positive desire. Whatever you constantly desire will eventually come to pass. You need five ingredients to fulfill any desire.

Ingredients for fulfilling your desire

D = Determination

Determination is explained separately, on the next page.

E = Enthusiasm

Enthusiasm is the drive to advance. It instills an "I can" attitude. Opportunities won't wait for you; you must seize every opportunity God presents you. Enthusiasm energizes you, and inspires others to want to join your journey team.

S = Strategy

Once you have a goal, you direct your actions towards achieving it. It's like knowing your destination and needing a map to find your way there. Strategy is about planning on how to arrive there.

As someone once said, "If you fail to plan, you are planning to fail." Strategy builds your confidence and prepares you to face obstacles positively along the way. It involves learning how to apply your available resources in order to accomplish your mission.

I = Intelligence

Intelligence involves gathering the information and knowledge needed to achieve a goal. Often, what we require is more knowledge rather than finances. Intelligence provides ideas on how to implement strategies. A wise person observes and learns from others without incurring costs. It involves applying thoughts to create solutions.

R = Relax

Relaxation is a forgotten art ithese days. People do not know how to relax. They are stressed about everything because they don't trust God. They think they have to be in charge all the time, otherwise things won't work out the way they want. We need to learn to relax. Our dream will not come true overnight. It is a process, and thus it is a long journey.

We need to learn to enjoy the trip while we are on our way. Many wait to reach their goal to relax and to be happy. God wants us to rest in Him. This is why the Bible says, "though we walk through the valley of the shadow of death I will fear no evil." Psalm 23:4.

This should be the confession of a soul who fears the Lord. If we begin to get stressful and irritated when we get a flat tire, we have a little hope when the flood comes.

The Bible says in Jeremiah, "if we are weary running with men, then how do we run with the horse. If the wilderness makes us weary what will we do when the Jordan floods?" (Jeremiah 12:5).

E = Example

An example is learning from others who have gone before you. As the Bible states in Hebrews chapter twelve: "Therefore we also, since we are surrounded by so great a cloud of witnesses, let us lay aside every weight, and the sin which so easily ensnares *us,* and let us run with endurance the race that is set before us,"

If you are open to learning from the experiences of others, it can spare you a great deal of trouble. Why repeat the same mistakes when you can learn from those around you?

Many fail along the way because they don't have a good example to emulate. While experiences may differ from person to person, the underlying principles remain consistent across generations.

Determination

This is the ability to stay on your path no matter what happens. Determination can turn every obstacle into an opportunity.

It serves as a bridge to cross many rivers. It acts as a raft to navigate challenging tides. It functions as a sail to guide you to your harbor. It serves as a compass when you feel lost. It provides energy when everyone else is tired. It enables you to keep working while others take a rest or a break. The most important thing is, that determination will prevent you from making excuses.

Nothing can stand against a determined soul—not even Mount Everest itself. Many merely have wishbones instead of backbones. All inventions and billion-dollar businesses begin with a single desire or idea. However, they combine that desire with determination.

Once you are determined to achieve something, you must have self-discipline to stay the course.

Self-Discipline

Discipline is the practice of self-control. Self-discipline will give stability and consistency to your mission. Many have desire and short-lived determination, but they lack the discipline to remain motivated.

Joseph achieved his dream, not by speaking in tongues or fasting, but by self-control.

You can have all the qualities that a person can ever have, but without self-control, you are like a tamed elephant that doesn't know how big and strong he really is.

When everything seems low and hopeless and you still keep doing what you are supposed to be doing, that is called self-control. You are not controlled by any outside force, but you are controlled from within yourself.

Your emotions and will are focused on the one thing you want to do with your life. With discipline, you will be consumed by your dream. Many people struggle with this third stage. They desire, determine, and begin something, but when storms and winds blow against their dream, they retreat and give up. They lose the prize, not because they didn't start the game, but because they lacked the discipline to stay the course and see it through to the end.

The biggest enemy of your dreams is not the devil, nor your spouse or in-laws. It is you! The greatest battle to be won is not in the heavens, but within yourself. If you can win the battle inside and conquer yourself, heaven will be on your side.

A lack of discipline keeps many champions hesitating in the makeup room. They are not ready to step out yet, as they are still trying to pull their acts together.

The first step toward achieving your dream is mastering yourself. The most undisciplined army is God's army on earth. They are all waiting for God to provide something before they take further action.

Mastering yourself means taking control of everything happening within you and around you. This is called dominion.

Many people make excuses for the way they are and how they do things. In reality, they just don't want to accept responsibility and improve. The worst enemy of your dream is your own undisciplined self.

Only a small percentage of people have removed the limits off themselves and, in doing so, gained a few lines in the pages of history.

History-makers are those who are willing to believe in what others fear to embrace. History-makers are those who act on what others merely dare to discuss. They are the individuals who are prepared to think what others can only imagine or dream about.

There are numerous examples around us. You cannot tell David that a stone can't kill a giant. You can't tell Moses that the Red Sea can't be parted. You can't tell Joshua that the walls of a fortified city can't be brought down by a shout. Until the Wright brothers came along, everyone else thought flying was impossible. Until Tenzing and Hillary arrived, everyone believed that Mount Everest couldn't be conquered. There exists an endless list of people who made possible what others thought was impossible.

Have you ever asked yourself, "What is my purpose? What is my dream? And what was I born to achieve?"

Ruth not only desired to go with Naomi, but she was determined to accompany her, no matter the struggles she would face.

Your promotion in life depends on how you respond to the struggles you encounter. How do you react to the negative aspects of life?

Your success or failure in life is defined by how you manage the obstacles you face. Every challenge that you encounter in life after committing yourself to God is not meant to destroy you; rather, it is sent from God to transform and strengthen you.

Birds fly against the wind's resistance. While resistance is what tires them, it is also what enables them to keep flying.

Are you ready to go against all odds in life? Are you ready to stand up and say, "Yes, it is possible," when everyone else claims it is impossible?

Ruth 1:22 says: "So Naomi returned, and Ruth the Moabitess her daughter-in-law with her, who returned from the country of Moab. Now they came to Bethlehem at the beginning of barley harvest."

They arrived in Bethlehem at the start of the barley harvest, indicating the time and season of their arrival. Timing is crucial in life. Once lost, time is something you can never regain, and it will not wait for you.

Where you find yourself in life today is very important, because God has appointed it. Do not dwell on the time you spent yesterday or the better time you hope to experience tomorrow; today is the perfect moment.

Time is one of the most precious gifts that God has bestowed upon humanity. Everything you possess in life today is the result of how you have utilized your time. Money is merely a reward for how you spend your time. The way you manage your time determines who you will become tomorrow.

If Ruth hadn't arrived in Bethlehem during the barley harvest, she wouldn't have ended up in the lineage of Christ.

Did you know that many people regret missing opportunities because they failed to arrive on time? One thing that amazes me is how many people watch sports on television. Many young people spend countless hours cheering for their favorite teams as those teams earn millions of dollars, while they themselves become poorer and lazier.

It's perfectly fine to watch games on TV after you've completed your life's responsibilities. You only get one moment at a time to advance and climb the next step on the ladder of your destiny. Don't squander opportunities; they may never return.

Some say that in the first part of your life, you waste opportunities, and they never come back. You cannot spend time like money. Your time is your currency, and you will be compensated for how effectively you manage it.

Everything under the sun has a purpose, and every purpose has its season and time. Seasons may return, but time will never come back. If you study the lives of those who achieve great things, you will find two key elements: order and punctuality.

Ruth 2:2: "So Ruth the Moabitess said to Naomi, "Please let me go to the field, and glean heads of grain after him in whose sight I may find favor."

Ruth asked Naomi for permission to go to work. That may sound strange; she didn't stay home and pray for God to bring the miracle to her.

Miracles happen for those who are willing to take the necessary action to do what God instructs them to do. No one in the Bible received a miracle just by praying. There was always action accompanying that prayer, which brought the miracle into their lives.

Many wait for the apple to fall into their lap when God is saying, "Plant the tree." Many people wonder how to get a day off from work when they start a new job. If your work feels dull and you can't wait to leave, please pray and ask the Lord for guidance. God's purpose for your life is not boring or exhausting. Fulfilling God's purpose will bring immense joy to your life.

Many wait until their parents or spouse push them to find a job.

Here is a single woman, in a foreign land, with no friends; who overcame her fears and stepped into her future. Ruth didn't have any prior contacts or phone calls. There were no job listings.

Ruth possessed a sense of adventure. She may have thought to herself, "Let me go out and see what I can find." She wasn't afraid to try something she had never done before.

Do you want to do God's will?

Then be prepared to go to places you've never been, and do things you've never done before. **Ruth stepped out of her comfort zone**. If you do what others do, you will get what they got. If you want something new in life that no one else has, then get ready to do something that no one else has done.

Ruth was not going to try it out and come back if she couldn't find anything. No, she was determined that until she found what she wanted, she was going to stay. She was not going to return empty-handed.

She was desperate to find help.

She was desperate to make a change.

She was desperate to build back her life.

It is easy for us to do something that we are comfortable doing. If you do what you usually do, you will get what you usually get.

Ruth came into the field that belonged to Boaz, one of Naomi's kinsmen. You may think she was lucky that she happened to be in that field. No, it was preparation meeting an opportunity. She was prepared and determined in her mind to try anything new that would bring a change into her life.

God works according to principles, not according to needs. If He worked according to the needs of people, there wouldn't be any poor people on the face of the earth today.

Many people pray for God to do the things they are supposed to be doing. They want Him to make them pray and, make them read their Bibles, and clean their bedrooms. No, that is not His job.

He will step in when you and I have done everything we are supposed to do.

"And she said, 'Please let me glean and gather after the reapers among the sheaves.' So she came and has continued from morning until now, though she rested a little in the house." Ruth 2:7

Ruth was a hard worker. She lingered a little longer in the house. Some of us need a half-hour break after two hours of work. In India, I've seen government officials start their day at ten o'clock in the morning, and by ten-thirty, they are already on a tea break. Some people request a raise and vacation after just two months in a new job.

Ruth paid respect to those who deserved it:

> So she fell on her face, bowed down to the ground, and said to him, "Why have I found favor in your eyes, that you should take notice of me, since I am a foreigner? Ruth 2:10

We live in a society where people often fail to grasp the importance of respect and honor. The fundamental values of honoring our parents, teachers, and elders are diminishing.

Do we show respect to those who deserve it, or do we continually believe that we are the best?

The Bible encourages us to regard others more highly, and to show respect in the presence of our elders. In Leviticus 19:32, it states: "You shall rise before the gray headed and honor the presence of an old man, and fear your God: I am the Lord."

Ruth 2:11-12 says:

> And Boaz answered and said to her, "It has been fully reported to me, all that you have done for your mother-in-law since the death of your husband, and how you have left your father and your mother and the land of your birth, and have come to a people whom you did not know before.
>
> The Lord repay your work, and a full reward be given you by the Lord God of Israel, under whose wings you have come for refuge.

Though she believed that no one knew her, Ruth earned an excellent reputation in the short period of her work life.

How many of us think that no one knows us when we are in a new place? We tend to relax a little, believing no one will find out. However, someone is always watching, no matter what you do or where you go. Jesus said that nothing is covered that will not be revealed (Luke 12:2).

Ruth was an industrious woman. Boaz ordered his servants to drop some of the corn purposely for her:

> Also let grain from the bundles fall purposely for her; leave it that she may glean, and do not rebuke her (Ruth 2:16).

> "If you do more than what you are paid to do, eventually you will be paid more for what you do." – Zig Ziglar

We tend to do less than what is required of us and then expect to be paid more. We forget the value of going the extra mile. As someone said, the last five minutes of your faith are crucial. In sports, the final moments determine the outcomes of champions.

It is not how you start something, but how you finish that matters. Any fool can begin anything, but only the wise know how to finish properly. Just like the five wise virgins, who were prepared and kept their lamps ready (Matthew 25:1-13).

Ruth finished the same day what she had started.:

> So she gleaned in the field until evening, and beat out what she had gleaned, and it was about an ephah of barley (Ruth 2:17).

She didn't delay until the next day. She didn't procrastinate. Don't procrastinate or put off tasks for tomorrow when you can complete them today.

Not many procrastinators ever accomplished anything significant in their lives. They keep saying, "I will start doing it tomorrow," and that tomorrow never comes.

How many things have you and I put off for the next day when we could have easily done them today?

Many people say *yes* to everything that comes their way, resulting in very little time to accomplish their tasks.

How many times have you had an argument with your spouse for not getting something done on time? Whenever you procrastinate, you are putting yourself on the losing team.

Ruth could have easily left the threshing for the next day because she was gleaning all day long under the scorching sun. She could have made an excuse to Naomi, saying, "I am just tired." Instead, she brought the grain back home, and they had a nice dinner. How many of you paid late fees on your bills when you could have sent them on time?

Ruth was thoughtful of others:

> Then she took it up and went into the city, and her mother-in-law saw what she had gleaned. So she brought out and gave to her what she had kept back after she had been satisfied (Ruth 2:18).

She ate what Boaz gave her, kept the rest, and brought it home for Naomi. She was not selfish.

I believe that was the day the breakthrough began in Ruth's life, when she gave Naomi a portion of food meant for her to eat. Concerned for her mother-in-law and showing her kindness, God in heaven came down to help her. I believe that when she gave that portion to Naomi, the power of poverty was broken and removed from her life.

God loves people who act with compassion, kindness, and mercy, regardless of culture or creed, because that is His nature.

> Then Naomi said to her daughter-in-law, "Blessed be he of the Lord, who has not forsaken His kindness to the living and the dead!" And Naomi said to her, "This man is a relation of ours, one of our close relatives (Ruth 2:20)."

Notwithstanding, Naomi was a fair-weather believer (Ruth 1:20, 21). They change with the weather. One day, they are excited and fully supportive of God, while the next day, you will find them feeling defeated, because something didn't go their way. They can be dangerous to be around. Today, they will shout Hosanna for you; and tomorrow, they may shout to crucify you.

Many churchgoers are happy when everything is going well for them and the church. However, when testing times arrive, they are often the first to run out the door. They will stick with you as long as their needs are met, but the moment things don't go their way, they will abandon you.

Ruth was a woman of great endurance:

> So she stayed close by the young women of Boaz, to glean until the end of barley harvest and wheat harvest; and she dwelt with her mother-in-law (Ruth 2:23).

If Ruth had stopped during the middle of the harvest, saying she had enough for the season, she would have missed out on God's best for her. The verse above says, "She kept fast." She didn't take a day off by calling in sick. She didn't look for an easy miracle or sign from heaven.

Ruth was there at her workplace, whether it was hot or cold, windy or stormy. She didn't keep changing fields to glean. She didn't accept the offer of free food. She didn't quit by saying, "I have been working here this long: maybe I won't find a man for me in this field, so let me go to the next one."

Some people change their church and job every six months. They cannot grow in the same place where God has planted them. We miss many blessings because we do not endure to the end. As Scripture says, "The end of a thing is better than its beginning" (Ecclesiastes) 7:8).

Ruth was a woman of complete obedience:

> Then Boaz said to Ruth, "You will **listen**, my daughter, will you not? Do not go to glean in another field, nor go from here, but stay close by my young women (Ruth 2:8).

There is a difference between partial obedience and complete obedience. With God, partial obedience is disobedience. King Saul had to learn this the hard way. He lost the kingship, anointing, and

God's favor in his life because of his partial obedience. An evil spirit tormented him because he was trying to please God through partial obedience.

It is very important how we hear God's voice. You may be spending all you have on something God hasn't spoken to you about. When things don't go the way they are supposed to go, then you get mad at God.

It is easy to obey as long as it is within your comfort zone, and it makes sense. What if God tells you and me something like He told Jonah?

Do we obey our spiritual leaders and parents? What if they are wrong? Jesus obeyed His parents for thirty years. The Bible says in Hebrews 5:8 that though He was the Son of God, He learned obedience by the things which He suffered.

Ruth was kind till the end:

> Then he said, "Blessed are you of the Lord, my daughter!
> For you have shown more kindness at the end than at
> the beginning, in that you did not go after young men,
> whether poor or rich" (Ruth 3:10).

It is easy to show kindness to someone when you see him or her for the first time. When a guest comes to your house, the first two days, you will treat them like a king. What about a week later? Will you have the same attitude towards them that you had in the beginning?

Ruth was not like that. She didn't move out of Naomi's place as soon as she found a source of income. Neither did she kick Naomi out of the house by saying she was an *old-school graduate*. Rather, she was kinder at the end than in the beginning.

God is kind to you and me even when we mess everything up. That is why we are alive today.

Ruth was a virtuous woman, a woman of honor:

> And now, my daughter, do not fear. I will do for you all that you request, for all the people of my town know that you are a virtuous woman (Ruth 3:11).

I have seen arrogant women who don't submit to authority or to their husbands.

Ruth was a woman who lived from within. She knew what she wanted, and she didn't let any distractions come her way. She was focused and committed.

Proverbs 31:30 says: "Charm is deceitful and beauty is passing, but a woman who fears the Lord, she shall be praised."

When Boaz recognized her faithfulness and dedication to her work, he promoted her. Ruth received three promotions along with raises during her first week on the job (Ruth 2:14-16; 3:15). What an incredible woman!

Also he said, "Bring the shawl that is on you and hold it." And when she held it, he measured six ephahs of barley and laid it on her. Then she went into the *city* (Ruth 3:15).

In the verse above, we see Boaz giving her six times more than she could earn in a single day's work.

If you remain faithful and fulfill God's purpose for you, He can provide in one day what you cannot achieve in an entire year. He is a God of abundance. As the Bible states in Ephesians 3:20: "Now to Him who is able to do exceedingly abundantly above all that we ask or think, according to the power that works in us,"

Every privilege or blessing carries a responsibility. We like blessings, but not the responsibility that comes with them.

Ruth's fourth promotion was the greatest—it was for her to become the co-owner of the field that she was gleaning from.

I believe it was her heart and character that attracted God's attention. She became an unforgettable woman, not because of the favorable circumstances. She didn't try to become like someone else. She kept her identity and followed her uniqueness. That was the secret behind her achievement. She became the grandmother of David, who was the greatest king of Israel and great grandmother of Jesus Christ.

Ruth broke every limitation and boundary in both the natural and in the spiritual realms. As a Moabite she was an outcast, but activating kingdom principles in her life, caused her to obtain favor with God and man. This is what happens in our lives when we break off the spirit of poverty from us.

CHAPTER 7

Understanding Your Uniqueness

Once you understand the principles of God's favor, the next thing you need to understand is your uniqueness. You are created uniquely and for a specific purpose. Only when you understand your uniqueness will you be able to identify your specific assignment!

You see in the Bible that God interacts with each individual uniquely. When you examine the Bible closely, you'll find that God never acts in the same way twice. He never communicates with two people exactly alike. When you take a closer look at the Bible, it's evident that God never performs something the same way twice. He always speaks to different individuals in distinct manners.

You don't see any repetition of the manner in which God used the people in the Bible. If you look at the Body of Christ today, everyone is comparing themselves with each other. Everyone is telling others to do what they are doing. Religion produces copies, in the kingdom there are only originals.

This is one of the main reasons many self-sabotage their callings or assignments. The moment God tells them to do something, immediately they go to someone else to ask for their opinion on the matter. Their friend or relative never did anything significant or outside the norm, so they give their limited opinion and thus talk them out of God's assignment.

You see in the Word that God spoke only to Abraham to sacrifice his son. There was only one burning bush. He spoke through the donkey only once. He dealt with each person differently and spoke to them differently.

Hence, you cannot take those once-off experiences and establish doctrines out of them. God always likes to do new things. God is never boring, and never gets old. God is a revolutionary. He likes to do things to revolutionize man's ways and traditions.

Man thinks based on their experiences and examples. It is difficult for mankind to accept or adopt change. He always likes to do things the way they have always been done.

God always does the opposite to the way we've always done things. His ways are always new. He never does things by comparing it to what was done before. So, whenever God does something, it is difficult for man to accept, simply because that was not the way it was done before.

Whenever God spoke to people to do something, they always got confused, wondering why He asked *them* to do it. Many have missed God's best for that one reason.

Notwithstanding, there were a few in the midst of it all, who chose God's way of doing things. They attempted to follow His Word. He backed it with His power, and they accomplished great and mighty things.

Those who dared to follow God's commands never failed because He backed these up. People often try to do things the same old way, raising their children in a uniform manner. Humanity tends to follow the crowd in everything they do.

Let me tell you, God has a specific way of dealing with you. You cannot impose that on another person. He doesn't want you to impose that on anyone else. He doesn't want you to study what others are studying because you are unique; besides, God has given you distinct talents, and a specific purpose.

Your relationship and your walk with your heavenly Father are unique. No one can have it the same way. When Paul asked us to follow him, he was not talking about day to day living or how he prayed. He was talking about his unwavering commitment and dedication to the Lord and his calling. He asked us to emulate that.

For your marriage, your ministry, and raising your children, God has a specific design reserved just for you.

Many people attempt to emulate others, leading to a multitude of duplicates and very few originals. Whether it's your marriage, your ministry, or bringing up your children, God has a unique plan tailored specifically for you. Yet, so many try to imitate others, resulting in numerous duplicates and only a few originals.

One of the main reasons why this world seems chaotic, and the church appears powerless, is that people are trying to fit themselves into roles or positions that God never intended for them.

Everyone wants to belong and feel accepted. Most of the time, they will try to find the easiest way to get comfortable with their life at an early age. After spending twenty or thirty years in one place doing the same thing, they are no longer prepared to take any risks, and their faith muscle gets weak.

Once in a while, when an anointed preacher comes through the town, as long as they are under his anointing, they will jump up and dance, but the next day they will snap back like a rubber band to their old lifestyle.

God's eyes are not running to and fro on the earth, looking for people with needs. His eyes are looking for those who is ready to do something new, like Peter who was willing to step out of the boat and walk on the water with Him.

Have you ever been in a situation where an opportunity was presented to you, and you knew you were supposed to accept it, but from a natural perspective, it looked so impossible, nor made any sense? That was God trying to get your attention.

God doesn't make cheesecake or pancakes. He makes the milk and wheat: now it is your responsibility to make the cake you like. Many people pray to God to send pancakes while God reminds them there is pancake mix in their pantry closets.

ONE OF THE MOST STARTLING THINGS THAT I FOUND

Do you want to know one of the most surprising and startling things that I found in the Bible?

God never gave any free money to anyone in the Bible. Whenever a person had a financial need, He always showed them the way to make money.

For example, the prophet Elisha, whom God placed under the care of a poor widow, instructed her to go and borrow jars from her neighbors and pour the oil she had into them. He gave her an idea to start a business (2 Kings 4:1-7). One time, Peter needed to find money to pay the tax, and Jesus told him to go catch a fish.

Every time God blessed someone, there was "work" involved in obtaining it. He wants people to be responsible and think critically. Many in the church today fast and pray for free money.

As one of your brothers in Christ, I want to tell you, that most of the time, God will reveal *a way* for you to make money. So, don't be surprised if God gives you a business idea when you ask Him for money. It is His will.

God gave the Promised Land to the people of Israel. The land was known as the land that flowed with milk and honey. But do you know what it takes and how much work is involved in caring for, herding, and feeding cows; and then harvesting honey from bees? Handling bees can put you in danger if you're not careful. Milk doesn't just flow from cows, nor does honey flow from bees. God wanted them to work and cultivate that fruitful land. The same applies to you and me.

RISKS, CHALLENGES, AND RESPONSIBILITIES

Today, people like no risks, no challenges, and no responsibilities. God's way is just the opposite. He loves people who are responsible and take risks—by trusting in Him. He loves people who are moving ahead with the ideas He is imparting to their hearts through His Spirit.

God is a God of purpose. He does everything with a purpose. Once you become a child of God, everything that happens in your life has a hidden divine purpose.

Not every challenge and failure is from the devil. The devil cannot even move his finger without God's permission.

To obtain God's best in your life will always cost you something. The higher you want to move with God, the greater the challenges will be. How far you want to go with God depends on how much you are willing to change. It is like walking on water. It is not by sight, but by faith.

God loves you so much that He wants you to have His best. Most of the time it won't come in the ways you calculate. God's ways are higher than your ways, and His thoughts are higher than your thoughts. For this reason, it is very important to stay close to Him, so that you can hear what He is saying to you.

WANTED, IMPORTANT, AND APPRECIATED

Every person needs to feel wanted and important. They want to be appreciated too. And, if they don't get that, they will get mad, depressed, and discouraged; and then they stop living the God-kind of life.

If you feel discouraged and unmotivated you may need to check your life to see whether you are trying to fit yourself into a place where you are not supposed to be.

BIRTHING A DREAM

A dream is never bought, caught, sought, or taught. It is birthed. A dream from God was planted in your heart when you were born.

Whether you call it a purpose, a vision, or a dream, God Almighty deposited it in you in seed form when He formed you in your mother's womb. That seed needs to grow, and if it needs to grow, it needs the proper environment.

The growth of a seed depends on the environment in which it is planted. This is why some people are not fruitful where they are. It doesn't matter how hard they try; they are simply not meant to be there.

Often, a geographical change is necessary for effective growth, meaning that one needs to be transplanted.

Most people who made a significant difference, whether in biblical times, modern times, or postmodern times, experienced a period of separation from their kin for a while. Examples include Jesus, Moses, Abraham, Joseph, Daniel, Esther, and many others.

Each of these individuals required a change of scenery in order to prepare themselves to be effective. Not all seeds thrive just in any soil. Different seeds need specific environments and climates. Mango seeds cannot grow in areas with heavy snowfall. Each country has its own native fruit tree that cannot thrive elsewhere.

Many people make the mistake of saying, "If God has a plan for my life, it will come to pass regardless of where I am or what I do; I just need to wait for it to unfold."

Hey there, let's get real! You've been waiting so long, and your life is becoming more and more chaotic! You don't feel inspired, and you keep questioning God. That doesn't sound like you're in God's will. Are you?

CHANGE IF YOU WANT TO BE FRUITFUL

Your dream won't become a reality without hard work, just as a baby won't grow by itself. The baby needs constant attention and care, just like your God-given dream. If you want to be fruitful, you need to change.

When a seed starts germinating, it goes through tremendous changes in its shape and structure. As it alters its shape and form, it may look different, but it is changing for the better. You will undergo the same experience when you seek to fulfill God's purpose for your life.

It can be a painful experience. You won't fit in with other seeds anymore. You start to stand out in the crowd. You are different. You think differently. You view things differently. No one understands you.

This is a critical stage where you are unsure of what is happening with you and what you will become.

So many people will draw back and try to remain the same because of fear of the unknown and criticism from other people. Your friends and relatives will try to scare you by saying you are not going to make it. They have not done anything worthwhile with their lives, so they are not qualified to give you any advice.

At least you were a seed before. Now, you've lost that identity. You've become a loner, with very few people to talk to. There are only two things we can trust during this season: God and time.

One day the seed will grow and start producing fruit that are useful to many. Even those who criticized you in the beginning will come back to join your team. They will look at you and say, "We should have done the same thing, but now it is too late to start something new."

Jesus was rejected by His people. He came to His own and they did not accept Him. His own family was upset with Him because they couldn't figure Him out. He didn't fit in with the crowd.

People will always love you and accept you as long as you are what they want you to be; but, the moment you try to be yourself, they will turn against you.

People said Jesus was demon-possessed when He began doing what He was meant to do. The moment He started fulfilling His purpose, He faced enemies trying to stop Him.

The fruit He bears now is worth the shame and ridicule He endured. Aren't we proud of what He went through, knowing it allowed us to be accepted into the Kingdom of God?"

The Apostle Paul said in 2 Corinthians 4:17, "For our light affliction, which is but for a moment, is working for us a far more exceeding *and* eternal weight of glory,"

THE SEED PRINCIPLE

The secret of fruitful living is to understand the seed principle. God said in Genesis 8:22, "While the earth remains, seedtime and harvest, cold and heat, winter and summer, and day and night, shall not cease."

We can be confident in God's Word, knowing that what He said is true and will stand the test of time.

In all the seeds you plant, the fruit is predetermined. If you plant an apple seed, you will reap apples, not oranges. However, there are two seeds in life that you can sow and expect a different harvest from: money and time.

God has given you the power to make this choice. When you buy something, you know about the product and what you will receive. You decide harvest.

The Bible says in 2 Corinthians 9:6: "But this I say: He who sows sparingly will also reap sparingly, and he who sows bountifully will also reap bountifully."

When you sow money into God's kingdom, it is He who decides the harvest. As human beings, we always like to be in control. That is why we don't like to give to the Lord, because we are not sure what and when we are going to get as the harvest. This all changes if you know God and how He operates.

God doesn't expect anything from you that He didn't first place within you. He will never ask for more than you can accomplish. If God requires something from you, it means it is already within you.

God is not a God who expects to harvest where He has not sown. He doesn't expect you to bring Him apples if He has given you the seed for oranges.

Somehow, we hold this intriguing notion about God—that He is unfair and demands something from us that He has not first provided.

If God is asking you to do something, know that He has already deposited within you the seed, the qualities, and the blueprint. You need to nurture that seed and care for it.

He doesn't want you to traverse seven seas in order to obtain something to get started.

Moses felt hesitant and frightened when God asked him to go to Egypt and deliver His people. He believed he didn't have what it took to be a deliverer.

God asked Moses, "What is in your hand?" Moses replied, "A staff." Well, that was more than enough. Everything you need to fulfill God's call is already in you or with you right now.

Joseph thrived even while in prison. That suggests whatever he needed for his prosperity was with him. David didn't attempt to create a weapon to defeat the giant; he recognized what he had—a sling and a stone—and used it to slay Goliath.

Most of the wars won in the Old Testament were not achieved by might or power, but by utilizing what was available to them under the guidance of the Holy Spirit. Jericho fell with a shout. Samson killed a thousand men with a donkey's jawbone. Gideon defeated the Midianites using torches and pots. Jehoshaphat overcame the enemy through praise and thanksgiving. The examples continue endlessly.

Unless you utilize what God has already provided and maximize it, He will not grant you more. Unless you learn and maximize it, He will not provide you with additional resources.

This lesson is evident in the parable of the talents in Matthew 25:14-30. The Lord rewarded the servant who invested and multiplied his talents. The one who failed to use what he had, had his talent taken away and given to the one who was already actively using his own talents.

The more you wait and do not use what the Lord has given you, the Lord will take what you have and give it to somebody else. God has to accomplish His purpose in His time, so if you are not willing to use what He has given you, He will find someone else who is ready to do what He says to do.

Many people do not recognize what God has deposited in them. They always look to other people and think, "If only I could get what he has."

One of the reasons you are not able to find what God has deposited in you is because it is in seed form. It won't be visible to the natural eyes, but in the spirit, you can feel your baby leaping inside of you.

Many people feel unimportant and neglected because they rely on what they see and fail to listen to the voice of their spirit. Every person born on this earth has a deposit from God within them, a pearl of great price, but they need to discover it.

To find that pearl of great price, one must dig through tons of dirt.

When I was a teenager, I felt useless and neglected, believing I could accomplish nothing with my life. I was discouraged and overwhelmed by despair. I felt depressed and hopeless as I observed others with great talents that I lacked, unable to see anything good within myself.

I did not understand my worth. I never heard a positive or affirming word from my parents. My father used to call me all kinds of filthy names except the name he gave me when I was born. My self-worth and confidence were nonexistent. Fear and insecurity were consuming me.

That was a time when God was shaping and transforming me. He was working within me, though I didn't know the outcome, which left me feeling lost and hopeless. It was a terrible period. But thankfully, God helped me through what I was experiencing at that time.

Conversely, the enemy will try to take from you what he hasn't invested in you. This is known as *Pharaoh's principle*. He will demand that you produce more than what he entrusted you with.

Have you ever wondered why God blesses some people abundantly while giving so little to others? In the parable of the talents, found in Matthew 25:14-30, we learn that God gives each person a measure according to their capability. If God has entrusted you with something, He expects you to use or invest it in order to gain more. On the final day, no one can blame God that their life was fruitless because they did not receive anything from Him.

One of the principles that God functions under is sowing and reaping. Proverbs 29:18 says, *"Where there is no vision the people perish..."* Vision refers to seed.

Imagine a world without seeds. God compares children to seed. The Bible uses terms such as 'seed of Abraham,' the 'seed of Jacob,' or the 'seed of the righteous.'

From now on, instead of mentioning *purpose, vision, plan*, or *dream*, we will use the word *seed*. The reason is, that a seed is something that needs to grow. If it remains the same, it doesn't produce any good.

The same way, your purpose, dream, and vision need to grow and produce the fruit that God intended. When you were born, God deposited a seed into your life.

What is a seed?

A seed is an entity that holds limitless potential to reproduce or multiply its own kind. As we often say, you can count the seeds in an apple, but you cannot count the number of apples that come from a seed.

You have unlimited potential waiting in you to be released. Your joy, your productivity, and your income - everything is included in that seed.

All that you ever need in your life has been deposited in that seed. It is not through the job you are doing that you are going to become prosperous; it is through recognizing your purpose, and fulfilling it.

If you examine a seed closely enough, it contains every detail and structure of the tree it is supposed to be. It has a blueprint of the tree.

It can absorb essential nutrients from the soil. That seed is fully prepared to produce its intended yield as soon as it is placed in the right environment.

Whatever you need to be productive and useful in the hands of God is within you. The Bible says you are born again by the incorruptible seed—the Word of God—Christ in you, the hope of glory, in whom all wisdom and knowledge are hidden in seed form (1 Peter 1:23; Colossians 1:27; 2:3).

"Counsel in the heart of man is like deep water,
But a man of understanding will draw it out." Proverbs 20:5

John 12:24 says: "Most assuredly, I say to you, unless a grain of wheat falls into the ground and dies, it remains alone; but if it dies, it produces much grain."

Many people remain the same for thirty or forty years. Others that you see after two or three years have gone through such dramatic changes in their lives that you can hardly recognize them.

A seed needs to be in the proper environment in order to grow effectively; otherwise, it will develop, but fail to produce the desired fruit.

You read about the parable of the seed in Matthew 13:3-8. Most refer to it as the parable of the sower, but the focus of this parable is not on the one who sows the seed, but on the seed itself.

We see in this parable, that the enemy targets the seed, not the sower. The enemy's purpose is to steal, offend, and choke the seed so that it won't yield fruit. In many lives, the enemy has effectively choked the seed, leaving them unable to function as God intends.

Every negative experience you've had in your life affects the fruitfulness of the seed. Every sin you've committed directly impacts the seed. The Bible states in 2 Corinthians 7:1, "...let us cleanse ourselves from all filthiness of the flesh and spirit..."

Whenever you do wrong, your spirit becomes defiled, and thus it needs to be cleansed. Unforgiveness and sexual sins defile your spirit more than any other.

Many people are unable to recognize the seed that God has deposited in their lives due to the things that have occurred in their past. You need to shake those off your life and find freedom in Jesus' Name.

Many people confess their sins, but struggle to achieve true freedom. The reason is, that even though God forgives, they don't truly repent and release their past experiences.

There is a difference between confession and repentance. *Confession* is what you express with your mouth, while *repentance* is a transformation that occurs in your mind. Repentance involves a change of mindset.

When you change your mindset, you don't revert to your old habits and thoughts. To forget your past experiences, you must cleanse your memories, which can only be accomplished by tearing down strongholds.

To learn more about this, you can read my book titled *Sin, Flesh, and the Devil.*

God desires your freedom not just in your spirit, but also in your emotions, will, body, and all areas of your life. Christ has paid the price for your complete freedom; however, the enemy will deceive you into believing that your current situation is the best you can ever achieve in life.

All you might need to do, is step out of where you are, and move to a place where your potential can flourish. If Ruth had stayed in Moab, she wouldn't have become who she was meant to be when she made the journey to Bethlehem. It certainly wasn't an easy road for her.

Mother Teresa would not have been the influential figure she is remembered as, if she had remained in Albania. Imagine if she had stayed home, fearful of the dirt and flies in the streets of Calcutta. No one would have known who Mother Teresa was.

William Carey would not have become the father of modern missions if he had stayed a cobbler in London. There were many other cobblers on the streets of London, but William Carey refused to be just another face in the crowd. Look at the impact he made on India and its Christian heritage.

Some of you are waiting for a sign from heaven and the perfect conditions to move forward in life. Others want to achieve greatness without sacrificing anything. They believe they are too perfect to get their hands dirty.

A seed has the power to absorb water and other minerals. It is uniquely designed to develop into a tree, with specific leaf sizes, branch lengths, and heights. It also embodies the fragrance of its flowers and their colors. It captures the taste of its fruit and the number of seeds contained within each piece of fruit, as well as their colors, flavors.

While I was typing this book on my computer, my three-year-old daughter Rachel came to me with a book and asked if I would read it to her. As I read that book to her, an idea blossomed in my heart. I don't believe I could have discovered a better story to complement what I'm writing.

The Legend of the Seed

This story will illustrate how God placed a seed (purpose) into our lives even before birth. The story is titled "The Legend of the Three

Trees," by George Taweel. I might've expressed it somewhat differently, as "The Legend of Three Seeds."

The story goes like this:

> Long ago, when God created the world, He made grass and seeds and trees.
>
> In a green valley, a hungry fox left behind an olive pit. From that pit, a new olive tree with beautiful wood sprouted and grew.
>
> Along a rocky shoreline, a stork dropped an acorn into a deep crack. From that acorn, a great oak tree took root and grew.
>
> High up on a mountainside, a clumsy goat knocked a log into a tree. The crash sent pine cones and their seeds tumbling to the ground. From one of those seeds, a new pine tree began to sprout.
>
> Each of the trees had great dreams of what it would eventually become. The olive tree dreamed that its beautiful wood could serve as a treasure chest decorated with sparkling jewels. The strong oak hoped to become a strong ship. Proudly, it would carry kings and queens across the waters. The tall, majestic pine hoped to always stay on the mountainside. There, it would forever point people to God.
>
> God had His own plan for each of the trees. The beautiful wood of the olive tree did not become a treasure chest. It became a feeding box for animals. But in that simple manager lay the greatest treasure of all time— God's only Son—Jesus.

The mighty oak tree did not become a great ship. It became a simple fishing boat. Yet that little boat carried Jesus—the King of Kings. In that boat, Jesus calmed a terrible storm with just a word.

The tall pine did not stay on the mountainside. It was made into a rough wooden cross. On that cross, Jesus died to save people from their sins. Ever since, the cross has reminded people of God's great love for them.

The dreams of the three trees came true. It was just not in the way they imagined. As with the three trees, God has a plan for each of us. And so we see, God's ways are not always our ways, but His ways are always best.

The story above tells each of us a great truth. God has designed you for a specific purpose, and all that it takes to become the person that God wants you to be, is implanted in you in seed-form.

Maybe it will take education, prayer, challenges, storms, or fasting to nurture that seed and make it grow.

You don't receive your seed from an outside source—not from your church, not from your parents, not from your friends, not from any books that you read, and not from your education.

Nevertheless, all of the above serve as ingredients to help your seed develop and grow.

Every seed has a covering or shell that protects it from external forces. Your body acts as a shell to safeguard the seed that God has planted in your life. God didn't give you your body for you to worship it. Whatever you spend the majority of your time on becomes an idol to you. Do not devote most of your time to caring for the shell, because that will perish one day. Instead, focus on developing the seed within.

Maybe you will start crying while you are reading a book when what you read touches that seed within you: or, maybe when you hear the Word being ministered, that seed in you will begin to kick you like a baby inside your womb.

You might receive ideas to preach, and new revelations from the Word, yet you never desired to be a preacher. Those are the signs that God is telling you to get prepared.

I felt that way. I never imagined I would become a preacher. I used to receive new revelations of the Word in my spirit; and I often thought, man, if I could share this with a pastor, he would preach about it—not realizing that one day I would be the one doing this.

When you go to bed, you feel it, and when you wake up in the morning, it wakes up with you. It is a desire that sticks with your heart. When you are in the shower, when you eat, it becomes your baby.

Finally, you will be possessed by that dream, and every minute and second of your life, you will be burning with it. You will feel like you are pregnant with something, and you just can't wait to give birth to it.

When you feel such desire, the first thing you need to do is to write it down (Habakkuk 2:1-3).

After you write it down, your job is to dedicate yourself to doing anything that is required of you in order to nurture that seed and make it grow.

You need to create an environment for that seed to grow, just like expectant parents prepare to have a baby. You need to be prepared to make some changes. You need to be ready to stay up some night hours, and travel on long trips. Be ready to change some diapers, and get your hands dirty.

God won't force you to make any changes; He will just give you a nudge in your spirit. Some of those changes won't be easy for the time being.

From now onward, your education, your reading, your friendships, your prayers, your church and your conversation should be geared toward the growth of that seed.

Imagine the changes Ruth was willing to embrace. She was entering a different culture. She might have had to adopt a different style of clothing—Moabites and Israelites did not share the same customs and culture at that time. There were varying tastes in food and cooking, a new language to learn, and differing manners.

The biggest thing was the religious setup of that day. In her day, women were generally not well respected. Some of us may think it was a piece of cake or a simple walk in the park for Ruth to become David's great grandmother; or, that it all happened by chance. No way. She paid a very high price to become what she became.

For us it is a story, but for Ruth it was life and death. Imagine what was going through her mind while she was on her way to Bethlehem. Are you willing to pay the price to fulfill your assignment?

CHAPTER 8

The Qualities of a God-given Seed

WHEN IT SEEMS UNATTAINABLE

The first thing you want to say is, "No, it can't be done." God gave Noah a mission to build an ark that was big enough to contain a pair of every living thing on earth. The reality was, that it had never rained before, and so the people of that day never knew what rain looked like. The very idea of rain couldn't fit into their mindsets.

Noah, living in a sinful and perishing generation, was the one man who found favor in the sight of God. He was the only person interested in knowing and fulfilling God's plan for his life.

In every generation, there are a few people ready to pay the price to fulfill God's purpose.

Many achieve great things and make lots of money, but that doesn't mean God blesses them. They are merely operating according to the principles God established in the beginning. Regardless of religion or faith, anyone who works according to God's principles will prosper.

The law of gravity will be in operation when a person jumps off the building, whether he is a Christian or not. Even in ancient Babylon, one of the ten rules of gold was to separate one-tenth of all the income you get and give that to bless others. That is tithing in God's Word.

Others were caught up in their own vain imaginations, having nothing to do with what God wanted them to do.

As of today, many can't fit the idea of God into their heart. That doesn't cancel out His existence. They think that if something had never happened before, it couldn't happen now. If they don't know about something, that thing could never exist or work out. If they couldn't do it, they thought no one else could. And if anyone else tries to do it, it is wrong. If it is something they cannot figure out, then it must be wrong.

God is not limited by human understanding and their inventions. We have not come anywhere close to His wisdom or power.

The people of Noah's day thought the idea of rain was a daydream. However, if God says something, it is established.

The way God works is through words—the principle of the spoken word. Whatever He needs, all He has to do is just speak it. If God spoke something, then it has to manifest in the appointed time. It cannot be altered:

> So shall My word be that goes forth from My mouth;
> It shall not return to Me void, but it shall accomplish what

I please, And it shall prosper in the thing for which I sent it. Isaiah 55:11

God doesn't need to use material things to do anything. Behind every work of God there are words. A word is an invisible substance with the power to manifest into a visible substance. A spoken word is an energy or power in motion. Jeremiah 23:29: "Is not My word like a fire?" says the Lord, and like a hammer that breaks the rock in pieces?"

There is nothing that the Word of God cannot burn, move, or shatter. There is no rock so hard that can stand against it.

Neither are there people or nations that are too strong to stop God from doing something. He can move anything in a moment. All He has to do is speak a word. We learn this from the story of the centurion in the gospel, whose servant was sick and asked Jesus to speak a word (Matthew 8:5-10). And when He spoke, his servant was healed.

There is no big problem in your life that God cannot solve. Right now, you can ask Him to speak a word to your problem in your family, work, or business.

Psalm thirty-three talks about the power of the voice of the Lord.

When God told Noah to build an ark, even though it seemed impossible to him, he believed it. He moved towards fulfilling it. When God tells you something, it will usually be something that no one else has ever done and you have never done before in your life.

This is why many people miss God's plan for their lives. They tend to compare things. They compare what they have with others. They evaluate their car against a friend's car and their house against their neighbors'. Even at work, they contrast their job with a friend who studied alongside them.

One of the most common mistakes ministers make is attempting to follow what God has instructed them to do based on the actions of other people or ministers.

That is not God's agenda for your life. He didn't make you to be like anyone else or to do as anyone else does. God starts a new history with every individual. Everyone has a track to leave behind him, but the principles are the same.

God doesn't like producing copies. He is in the business of making originals. Don't try to be a copy when you were created to be an original. Do not try to be a story when God is making you part of history.

The individuals who make a difference are those capable of believing in God's vision for their lives. Do not conform to this world. This is why Romans 12:2 states: *"And do not be conformed to this world, but be transformed by the renewing of your mind, that you may prove what is that good and acceptable and perfect will of God."*

That means this world is in the business of reproducing copies. Even in companies they make one blueprint of their product and one mold, and the rest you get are copies. You never get the original. The car you drive is not an original. Any electronic equipment that you have is just a copy.

God never used two people the same way, and neither did He create two people the same way, not even twins. Jesus didn't perform two miracles the same way.

He offers a new approach to your life. This is why you feel so lost. You don't belong anywhere, not in the crowd, and you end up feeling disappointed because you can't find anything you enjoy. This suggests that you need to uncover the blueprint from your creator.

God is not in the business of giving used stuff. He doesn't waste. He has something new for you—a way that no one else ever walked, and a life that no one else ever lived. Only you are fit to walk in that way.

God gave the exact plan to Noah concerning the ark—the length, breadth, height, and what kind of wood he should use.

God won't just give you a glimpse and trust you to figure out the rest. He knows that you will mess up without help; so, whenever God wants you to do something, he has detailed plans.

If you don't have everything you need, then wait until you get it. Because it is new, you won't have anyone to refer to or books to read to do research. You can search and study the principles but not the method. You can't research and find a new model of a car in the libraries; you need to invent one.

When God told Moses to build the Tabernacle, He gave him a step-by-step procedure because no one had ever built anything like that before.

Do you have a blueprint for the dream God gave you? The instructions will come from God, but some of the other details will come from other people.

God told Noah which wood to use, and then he needed someone to help him find that wood and cut it. Moses knew what was needed in the Tabernacle, but he couldn't do everything alone. In the same way, you need other people in your life to fulfill your God-given dream.

There are people who want to do everything by themselves. They are self-centered and want everything for themselves and are inconsiderate of the needs and feelings of others. They don't like to share the glory with anyone.

God gave the measurements: Now you need an engineer to cut the wood and make it the right size. God may have given you a vision to start a radio station. Now you need a person who knows how to do it.

You may have a vision to start an orphanage, but you don't have a building, or perhaps your neighborhood doesn't need one. It might be intended for another country, so you need someone to carry it out for you.

God doesn't provide a plan to a team; He gives it to an individual. Many churches and organizations remain stagnant because they believe God will communicate with their committee if He wants them to make a move. But that rarely occurs. If one person feels compelled to act because God has instructed him, others often won't support him, since God didn't speak to them. This is not how God operates.

He finds one man he can trust and communicates his plans to him. If he shared an idea with a group of people, he would encounter the same problem he faced at the Tower of Babel. People would begin building monuments for themselves and monopolizing the community and resources.

God didn't share his plans for the ark with Noah's family, but with Noah alone. There will be times when you need to stand up for yourself because it's just you and your dream on the playground.

Do not discuss God's plan for your life with other people to make it work or find ways to work it out. They will always try to divert you a little bit here and there because they didn't receive it in the first place. They have a lack of complete comprehension for what God is trying to do through you.

You may need an education, and God told you to go to this particular city or country to get it. When you discuss it with your brother or a family member, they will tell you why you should not go that far when the same education is available in your town at a lower expense. It will sound like a good idea, and if you listen to them and settle for convenience, you will miss the complete plan of God.

God may want you to go and preach the gospel to a particular group of people, and when you share that with your pastor, he will tell you why you should not go that far when you have people in your town who need to be reached with the gospel.

God is very particular about His plans. He demands complete obedience from you to the exact plan He gave you. If He told you to measure 8 cubits, He expects you to measure exactly 8, not 7.99, and if you still do it, you will be disobeying Him. If God told you to give $100 to a ministry and you gave only $99 while waiting for a miracle to come, let me tell you, there is little chance of that miracle ever manifesting.

GOD IS FAITHFUL TO FULFILL HIS WORD

Anything and everything or any person who stands in His way of performing His word will be removed quickly.

Saul lost his kingdom because he failed to perform God's command to annihilate the Amalekites. Then he presumed that he could sacrifice to God to please him after disobeying.

Do you have any sacrifice like that in your life?

Don't try to please God by doing extra work that He didn't ask you to do. After finishing exactly what He told you, then go the extra mile.

David lost Uziah because he tried to bring the ark in a cart when it was supposed to be carried on the shoulders of priests. Moses lost the chance to enter the Promised Land because he struck the rock instead of commanding it.

It's as if you've been building a palace all these years, and when it was finally ready, you couldn't even stay there for a day. All the effort and suffering you endured to create that palace were lost in a single act of disobedience. Thousands of Israelites lost their lives because they disobeyed God's word at various times.

God works according to the principle of details. Jesus said in the gospels to count the cost before you build the tower (Luke 14:28-30).

So, Noah didn't have to figure out from scratch how to build his ark, but he had the exact blueprint.

When you see a person who knows what he is doing, get around that person and learn as much as you can. You will learn from such a person what you won't learn in twenty years from a college education.

Even though God is not limited by time nor controlled by it, we are limited and controlled by it. He expects us to work within a time frame. As the Bible says, *"there is a season and time for every purpose under the heaven"* (Ecclesiastes 3:1). So, it is your responsibility to finish the job within time, so you won't be out of God's plan for your life.

Noah had to finish his work within a certain amount of time. The name Noah means "we shall rest from troubles."

A person's name is very important. You write your name more than anything else. You are conscious of your name day and night. Your name can have such an impact on your life and future. In the Bible, whatever the person's name was, that is what they became in their life.

You could become what your name means if you are conscious of your name all the time. If you name your son Dameon (demon in Latin), don't expect him to act like an angel of the Lord. God is very particular about your name. If He didn't like a person's name, or it didn't match with their destiny, He changed it. Why did He do it? Because they think and speak their name all the time and they could never become what God wanted them to be, like both Peter and Israel.

Peter's name was Simon, meaning unstable. Jesus knew that if he remained unstable, he couldn't trust Peter with His mission. He needed to change Peter's thinking process. The only way to do it was to change his name.

What impact does your name have on your life? What you think about most in your life is what you are going to become.

A good name is better than precious ointment... Ecclesiastes 7:1

If your name makes you feel inferior or holds you back, then you should consider changing it. God changed the names of eight people in the Bible because those names didn't reflect their purpose. Their parents named them incorrectly because they were unaware of their purpose.

Do you think it's impossible to accomplish what God has asked of you? Be patient for the details. He may not reveal everything to you all at once, but as you progress, He will gradually unveil things to you

THE PRINCIPLE OF DURATION OR SEASON

Another principle God works by is on the basis of the principle of duration or season. God didn't give Abraham the complete plan of where He was taking him. He had to tarry or stay in different places and get God's direction while en route.

He doesn't give you all of the details. He will give you the big picture, and as you take each step of obedience, He reveals the next.

Abraham had to make regular stops along the way and wait for God's guidance. He told him to go to a place where he would show him, but did not reveal all the plans at once.

If God has a plan for your life, He won't tell your neighbor or your friends. God will give some directions to parents in some cases, how to bring that child up, but not all of the plans.

Jesus was born to Mary, but she didn't understand completely what God was trying to do through her Son. It is mentioned in the Bible that she kept certain things in her heart, to reflect on later and see what they would become (Luke 2:51).

Other examples include John the Baptist and Elizabeth, Samson and his mother, and Samuel and Hannah.

It is our nature that we try to fill in the blanks when we get a hint of what God is going to do, and then we jump in and fill in the rest and try to do it; but it won't work out that way.

God enjoys making what men say is impossible possible. When a man says something can never be done, God walks in and shows them how it can be done. Whenever man said something was impossible, God showed them how it was possible.

It has happened throughout the past century. The Titanic was regarded as an unsinkable ship. They claimed that not even God could sink it; however, on its maiden voyage, God demonstrated how an iceberg could bring down their so-called unsinkable contraption.

According to Proverbs 18:21: "Death and life are in the power of the tongue, and those who love it will eat its fruit."

Sometimes it will be a painful experience. So, watch what you say with your mouth because it has power, and it could come to pass.

Noah believed that what God said would surely come to pass and he was counted righteous in his generation.

NO NATURAL RESOURCES

When God tells you to do something, He doesn't expect you to use the resources that you have at your disposal. Most likely, you won't have what He is asking. All that you need to fulfill His plan, comes from Him.

When a king sends his servant to accomplish something for him, he doesn't expect the servant to go and do all things at his own expense. If the king asks such a thing, he is an unreasonable king. The king will make all of the necessary arrangements for his servant, because he is at his command.

Dear ones, believe it or not, when you are at God's command, He will make your way straight (Proverbs 3:5-6). Trust in the Lord with all your heart; He will make your ways possible. Acknowledge Him in all your ways.

The Bible says that we are His ambassadors (2 Corinthians 5:20 and Ephesians 6:20). If you want to be an ambassador, you cannot be one in your own country. You need to go to a foreign nation. God has sent us as His ambassadors to this earth. It doesn't matter where you are born; you don't belong in that country.

I am not an Indian, and you are not an American or whatever nationality you are. When you die, you don't go back to the country where you were born, but you go to the country from where you came. The Bible says that our citizenship is not here but in heaven (Philippians 3: 20). We are here on this earth only for now.

If God sends you to do something on this earth, it is His responsibility to provide everything you need to accomplish His purpose.

When God created Adam, first, He prepared everything a man would ever need in his life to live and fulfill His purpose; then He brought Adam to the Garden of Eden.

If you are wondering where you will find the resources to fulfill your dream, they were prepared before you were born. You need to find them, and God will show you if you follow His dream.

When a king sends his servant to accomplish his purpose, he arranges for people to meet with the servant when he arrives at the appointed place. They will treat the servant as if they were dealing with the king himself, showing him the same respect and regard. Similarly, the king will engage with people at his own level, demonstrating his authority and dignity in every interaction.

As a servant of the King, you are protected and guarded by his forces. If anyone tries to do you any harm, it is the king's responsibility to protect you and enforce that arrangement.

Nehemiah served as a cupbearer to a king, a crucial time of preparation for him. Upon hearing about the dire situation in his homeland, the people, and the temple; the seed that God had planted in his heart began to stir within him.

This is why we read in the Bible that the Spirit of God began to move individuals like Samson, Saul, David, and others. Being a wise man, Nehemiah took the time to separate himself in prayer and fasting before receiving God's direction.

Many people don't wait for God's plan and timing. As soon as they hear or feel something God wants them to do, they jump in and try to accomplish it. When they fail, they return and claim it was not from God. Initially, they insisted it was from God, but just because they messed it up, suddenly it isn't.

Wait a minute—God is faithful to His Word; He doesn't change His mind. Complete trust is essential. Anything you attempt without the Lord's guidance and help is destined to fail.

God will make the necessary arrangements to fulfill His plans. He transferred wealth from the resources of the king to provide Nehemiah with the means.

Are you waiting for money to arrive before starting something? Is money the problem or the obstacle that's holding you back?

I don't think so. It has never been about money. Your real problem is a lack of understanding of God's ways. God's challenge is finding someone who truly understands how He works.

Everything around you may appear hostile. You need to confront your inadequacies—physical, mental, familial, and other obstacles.

GREAT OBSTACLES TO OVERCOME

Overcoming great obstacles often involves situations like the following:

God wants you to be a musician, but you can barely sing.

- God wants you to be an ice-skater, but you have polio in both legs.

- God wants you to be a redeemer and sustainer of your family, but your own family kicks you out of the house (Joseph).

- God wants you to be the most outstanding leader, but you have a speech impediment and criminal record (Moses).

- God wants you to restore broken families, but your own family is in a mess (David).

- You are born to deliver the people from their sin, and they say you are born in sin (Jesus).

- God wants you to be the Savior of the world, but you are born in a manger to poor parents.

- God wants you to be the top person in the government, but you are in captivity in a foreign land (Daniel).

- God wants you to be the greatest reformist and revivalist, but you are a cupbearer for the king in a heathen land (Nehemiah).

- God wants you to be a great-grandmother of the King of kings and Lord of lords. But here you are, a widow and a child of an outcast (Ruth). Yet, here you are, a widow and a child of an outcast, like Ruth.

- God wants you to be the prime minister of the super-power nation of your time. Yet, here you are in prison, sweeping floors and eating hot dogs like Joseph.

- God wants you to be the man of the century, but you are a high school dropout (Einstein).

IT WILL ALWAYS BE PEOPLE-ORIENTED

God has placed a seed in your life, not only for your own blessing, but primarily for the blessing of others. He has instilled that seed within you because He cares for your family and generations to come.

God gave a dream to Joseph, not for him, but for his family and for the nation.

God called Abraham and instructed him to go to a place that He planned to reveal. It was not for Abraham himself that God called him out, but for his descendants after him. The Bible states that he lived in the Promised Land as a stranger, not fully obtaining the promise (Hebrews 11:39); but he earned a good reputation because of his faith:

In the natural realm, you plant the seed not for the seed's sake, but to produce fruit. The seed has no purpose other than the fruit. The fruit exists to bless others. So, please don't catch yourself saying, "Me and my world." You are in this world to become a blessing to someone else.

God told Abraham that He would make him a blessing. Moses was called not for his great personality, but for the people in bondage.

As it is for the people, you will need other people to help you to develop and fulfill the dream that God has deposited in you. You can't do it all alone.

One quality of a God-given dream is that you need other people on your team to achieve your goal. Though God has planted the seed within you, you don't possess everything necessary to bring it to fruition.

For a seed to grow, it must be planted in the soil. It requires water and essential minerals in order to thrive. If the seed attempts to do everything independently, it will soon be vulnerable to being eaten by birds, moths, or rodents.

If God has called you to be a king, what good is a king without people to rule? Just because you are as sweet as sugar, no one can consume too much of it unless it combines with other ingredients.

JESUS CAME TO GIVE HIS LIFE AS A RANSOM FOR MANY

Every invention and discovery was never intended for the person who made it, but for countless generations thereafter. Every orchard was planted not merely for the orchard itself. Every rose that is in the garden is for you to enjoy its color and fragrance.

God's blessings are perpetual, just as His Word is. Therefore, you must keep your eyes and heart open in order to recognize and receive the people whom God is sending your way.

The devil also sends individuals to destroy the seed and divert you from your path, so it's essential to have the guidance of the Holy Spirit to discern who is from the devil and who is from God.

GOD IS A COMMUNICATOR

God likes to communicate with you first, before He tells anyone else. We see repeatedly in the Bible that God is saying to His people: "Let him who hath an ear, hear what the Spirit says." He desires to tell you what He is going to do with your life (Revelation 2:7).

Sometimes, if you are stiff-necked and rebellious, He tells others (Exodus 32:9, Acts 7:51). Most of the time though, He uses other people to confirm the Word that He has already spoken to you.

As you go ahead with God's plans for your life, you need repeated assurances from God to ensure you are on the right path. He will reveal step by step the things He wants you to do.

Abraham used to make stops and build altars. I believe he did that to confirm his paths and hear from God occasionally. God spoke to him through recurring events and progressively revealed the plan to him.

In Genesis 12:1, we read of the call of God coming to Abraham to get out of his country, his kindred, and his father's house to go to a land He was going to "show" him.

God didn't promise that He would "give" the land. In verse seven, God appeared to him and said He would give the land to his descendants.

In Genesis 13:14, we read, "The Lord appeared to him again and said that He is going to give the land to him and his descendants forever." God's plan was revealed to him progressively, gradually.

QUALITIES OF SELF-MADE PLANS OR PURPOSES

Self-made plans often display traits that obstruct their success and alignment with a divine purpose. These include the following:

1. Inconsistency

One day, you want to do something, and the next day, you are gravitating towards something else. For example, you may want to produce movies one day, and become a missionary the next.

2. Lots of Effort but Few Results

These plans often involve significant effort but rarely deliver the results you expect.

3. Unproductive

Despite all your hard work, the outcome is often fruitless, with no tangible or meaningful results.

4. Waste of Time and Resources

Pursuing such plans can waste valuable time, energy, and other resources, leaving you feeling drained and unfulfilled.

5. Self-Centered

Self-made plans are typically focused on what you can gain, rather than serving others or a higher purpose.

6. No Need for Supernatural Intervention

If a plan requires only your own abilities and doesn't depend on God's guidance or intervention, then it is likely not from Him. If you don't need God to accomplish it, it's not divinely-inspired.

Do you want to become everything that God intended for you to be? Then listen to Him, and not to other people. People will try to make you like themselves. What He has in mind for you, He has never done with anyone else.

God wants you to have a life that is fruitful and fulfilling—not filled with misery. You become miserable when you compare your life with others. You lose your uniqueness when you try to have what other people have or try to become like someone else. There are millions in this world today who lose their identities and uniqueness because they are trying to be like someone else, and they merge as drops of water in the ocean of mediocrity.

What I'm writing is not necessary for everyone, but for a select few like you who are reading this book. You are unique. Don't shy away from your differences; instead, embrace them as your individuality, and stand up as the person God intended you to be. Show this world who you truly are.

Make a mark in history. Create a lesson for others to learn from you. Craft a story that others can read. Paint a portrait for others to admire. Be an open book so that others can learn from you. Exude a fragrance that others can sense. Be authentic so that others can be themselves.

When you understand your uniqueness, life will never be boring. Life never gets old, because it is always new. Every day is a new day, and you should be happy because you have never lived that day before!

Do you want to be an original, or do you want to remain a copy of someone else?

People who made a difference in our lives did so because they chose to be different. They stood alone in the crowd when there was no one to support them. They dared to be different, and thus they left an impact.

Nothing happens by chance. I'm not trying to tell you to be a jerk or arrogant, but rather to be different and original for God and His purpose. When you truly want to fulfill your calling, you will stand apart from others. Your talents are unique, and your destiny is distinct.

Even though we all travel on the same bus, we will disembark at different points in life. You approach things differently. You see things differently. You are a unique creation of God, and therefore, God has a special purpose for you.

CHAPTER 9

Enemies of God's Purpose

WHY PEOPLE FAIL AT FULFILLING GOD'S PURPOSE FOR THEIR LIFE

So, there are as many reasons why people fail as there are failures. Here's just some of these.

The Spirit of Fear

This fear comes from a lack of faith. If there is one demon that keeps people bound from receiving the blessings of God, it is the spirit called *fear*. It was one of the first demons that entered mankind after committing the first sin in the Garden of Eden.

When God called out to Adam in the cool of the day, the first thing that came out of Adam's mouth was, "I was afraid" (Genesis 3:10). Since then, everyone born in the likeness of Adam is susceptible to that spirit.

The Bible says in 2 Timothy 1:7: "*For God has not given us a spirit of fear, but of power and of love and of a sound mind.*"

Every time you do something for the first time, or when you stand in front of people to speak, there's a feeling in your stomach that some call "butterflies." In reality, it is a demon of fear that makes you so uncomfortable.

The next thing Adam said was, "I was naked," indicating that he felt unworthy to stand before God. An inferiority complex stems from that demon of fear.

What would you do with your life if you were not "afraid" to fail?

The spirit of fear stops many from attempting great things for God. This spirit manifests in different ways in the lives of different people. Some are afraid of heights, water, people, darkness, speed, fire, and so on.

Childhood Experiences

Even before you were born, the devil tried to mess up your life so that you wouldn't recognize and fulfill God's plan for your life.

Every negative experience that happened in your life before you came to Christ had one purpose: to keep you away from God by cluttering your mind and defiling your spirit with knowledge and experiences that were contrary to God's Word. Due to this defilement, you become flawed and ineffective.

The abuses that children endure—sexual, emotional, and physical—had one purpose: to affect them deeply, to make them withdraw into themselves and become introverted.

There are more people with mental disabilities on the face of the earth today than those with physical disabilities. Not all are born that way, but the experiences they faced have made them captives. Many are prisoners of their past and their own circumstances.

They blame God for being unkind to them, only to realize sooner or later that it was they who were unkind to Him.

Jesus came to set the captives free and to bring freedom to those who are bruised (Luke 4:18).

The Devil is the Master of Deception

If you look back on your life, most of the experiences that affected your mind and spirit occurred when you were a child. Later, what you experienced were reflective responses to those earlier incidents. Those experiences set invisible parameters or boundaries on how far you could go with your life.

There are few who broke free from those limitations—who went on to do extraordinary things for God. Your childhood experiences laid the foundation upon which your life is being built.

The foundation determines the strength and height of a structure. It doesn't matter what you faced; you can break through any limitation and live a limitless life with God.

A Wrong Perception of God

Many do not give God the credit that they give to their big brother. If you want to fulfill God's plan for your life, you need to get Him out of the box you have placed Him in.

It doesn't matter how big you think God is; He is still bigger than your wildest imagination. All that tradition does is attempt to limit a limitless God. Many believe that God is overly strict, serious, and no fun to be around. They think God is just waiting for them to make mistakes so He can punish them afterward.

The Bible states that God is love (1 John 4:16). God is not angry with you. He loves you more than you realize.

You may wonder why all the wrong things happen in your life and why evil exists in this world. It is not because God is angry or evil; it is because mankind broke the order that God set for us to live by.

It's like jumping from the top of a five-story building and expecting not to get hurt. It would be foolish to think that, because you are disregarding the law of gravity. You can't blame God for the pain caused by your fall.

The same principle applies to every area of your life. God has established laws (regulations or teachings), statutes (customs or manners), precepts (directions or orders), and commandments (instructions or prescriptions) in His word for you to follow in order to be safe and productive.

When you rebel against these, you will face the consequences of that rebellion. All the evil in this world results from breaking God's order. He wants us to take responsibility for our actions.

God is not a complaint box, nor is He a trash can. He is Almighty and Sovereign, and He does whatever pleases Him (Psalm 115:3). So, please, stop blaming Him; and instead, get to know Him. He gets sweeter every day, and you will be blessed.

The Measure of Faith

What you attempt to achieve in life depends on the extent of your perception of God. If you believe He is great, you will receive great blessings; and if you view Him as being small, you will receive according to that measure of faith:

> For I say, through the grace given to me, to everyone who is among you, not to think of himself more highly than he ought to think, but to think soberly, as God has dealt to each one a measure of faith. Romans 12:3

I have heard people misinterpret this scripture because many thought they had faith according to the measure that Christ gave them.

Do you know how great Christ's measure is?

When a person gives gifts, he gives according to his capacity. When you buy a gift for someone, you buy according to your financial capacity and generosity.

Do you know that the Bible says the wisdom, power, and love of God are unreachable? God is so big that whatever He is and has is as limitless as Him.

Isaiah 40:12-13, 15-17 asks:

> Who has measured the waters in the hollow of His hand, measured heaven with a span and calculated the dust of the earth in a measure? Weighed the mountains in scales and the hills in a balance? Who has directed the Spirit of the Lord, or as His counselor has taught Him?
>
> . . .
>
> Behold, the nations are as a drop in a bucket, and are counted as the small dust on the scales; look, He lifts up the isles as a very little thing. And Lebanon is not sufficient to burn, nor its beasts sufficient for a burnt offering. All nations before Him are as nothing, and they are counted by Him less than nothing and worthless.

I heard this story about Alexander the Great:

> One of his childhood friends visited him one day. He sought him out because he was very poor and hungry, hoping to receive a meal to satisfy his hunger.

When Alexander saw him, he was moved with compassion and inquired about his life.

Upon hearing the need, Alexander responded, saying, "When I give gifts, I give according to my capacity.

I have just conquered a new country, and I have decided to appoint you as its governor."

We know that Christ is the King of kings and the Lord of lords, so when He gives you something, it is according to His greatness, not according to your pipe dreams.

The question is, are you ready to receive all that He has given to you?

Ephesians 1:19 says: *"and what is the exceeding greatness of His power toward us who believe, according to the working of His mighty power"*

Colossians 2:3 says: *"in whom are hidden all the treasures of wisdom and knowledge."*

The Bible says that you should be filled with all the fullness of God (Ephesians 3:19).

Instead, take your twisted mentality about God, and ask according to His greatness.

Psalm 2:8 says: *"Ask of Me, and I will give You the nations for Your inheritance, and the ends of the earth for Your possession."*

Ignorance

Ignorance is an illness from which people need to be healed. The worst aspect of this illness is that individuals are unaware of their condition. Those who suffer from this demon of ignorance do not recognize their lack of knowledge, because they are unaware of their own ignorance.

Ignorance of Spiritual Timing

God has appointed a time and season for everything in your life. The difference between time and season is that time is spent once and for all, and you won't get it back; however, if you miss a season, you will have the chance to experience that same season again.

God is a God of Second Chances

If you miss what He is trying to do with your life in this season, He will give you another. This is why we have fixed seasons throughout the year. The Bible says in Ecclesiastes 3:1 that: *"To everything there is a season, a time for every purpose under heaven:"*

Ignorance of God's Word

Many know the information in God's Word, but few understand the power of it. God's Word is not just a book; instead, it is God revealing Himself through the written word.

God created everything by the power of His Word:

"By the word of the Lord the heavens were made,
And all the host of them by the breath of His mouth.
Psalm 33:6

The Word of God is not the name of a book, but of a person; so, treat your Bible as you treat God; and believe what it says, as if it is God speaking to you:

He was clothed with a robe dipped in blood, and His name is called The Word of God. Revelation 19:11-13

Ignorance of Who You Are

The only creatures that do not accept the way God created them are human beings. That is why they need make-up and cosmetic surgery to cut, paste, and keep themselves looking different from how they are.

All other creatures are content with being happy and doing what they are supposed to do. Only human beings wonder and worry about these vanities.

The Bible says in Luke 3:38, "... *Adam was the son of God.*" (KJV)

Whatever is part of something, is that very thing. The kitten of a cat will grow into a cat; the calf of an elephant will become an elephant. Why do we think differently? If a candy is made with chocolate, that candy must be full of chocolate, right?

If the Bible states that we are the children of God, then our spirits must share the same qualities as God. That's why the Bible mentions that we are made in the image and likeness of God. You should be convinced of this truth with every fiber of your being.

The Bible says in John 1:12: "But as many as received Him, to them He gave the right to become children of God, to those who believe in His name:"

This is not an abstract truth. It is something you can and must experience in life on this earth. God is not saying this to make you feel good about yourself; He is saying it because you are what He says you are. Psalm 8:4-6 says:

> What is man that You are mindful of him, and the son
> of man that You visit him? For You have made him
> a little lower than the angels, and You have crowned

him with glory and honour. You have made him to have dominion over the works of Your hands; you have put all things under his feet,

No one can destroy God's plan for your life, your purpose, or your seed. No one can take that away from you. No one can kill you before God's appointed time. Here's the proof:

- Daniel—in a lion's den

- Shadrach, Meshach, Abednego—in a fiery furnace

- Paul—bitten by a snake and went through innumerable life-threatening troubles

- Jesus—various people attempted to kill Him many times

- Moses—all his male contemporaries were killed as new-born infants by the Pharaoh's order

There is only one force that is powerful enough to cancel God's plan for your life, and that is you—your willpower to make a choice or decision.

God will never change His mind concerning your life. His call and gifts are irrevocable. (Romans 11:29).

The devil can only cause diversions or delays in preparation, but not God's plans. Family and friends (1 Kings 13), lack of preparation, pride, and unbelief are some of the other influences that will hinder you from fulfilling God's purpose for your life.

You must be a risk taker. If you are afraid to take risks in your life, I doubt that you are going to make it.

CHAPTER 10

Fulfilling Your Calling

More than you want to know and fulfill God's calling for your life, God wants you to understand and accomplish it. More than you desire to know and fulfill God's purpose for your life, God desires for you to comprehend and fulfill it. Here's how you can proceed:

1. **Receive Jesus Christ as your personal Savior and Lord**

2. **Pray and meditate on the Word for daily direction**

3. **Divide your dream up into achievable goals**

4. **Stick to it**

Have you ever thought that if you just looked like someone else, you would be perfectly able to fulfill God's plan for your life?

This world is very good at depersonalizing individuals. Advertisements and models are geared towards causing people to want to look like someone else. They make you feel guilty and reject yourself because you aren't like someone else.

TRAINING FOR SUCCESS—GOD'S WAY

God's ways of training differ from how earthly systems operate. Before God uses you for His glory to fulfill His assignment through your life, you must go through certain stages in order to grow and mature. His focus is on your *spirit*, not your mind or muscles, as in worldly educational systems.

Here's what He wants you to focus on once you're connected to His purpose for your life:

a) **Separation**

b) **Preparation**

c) **Realization**

d) **Manifestation**

Separation

God will separate you from the people, systems, or traditions that you naturally follow. Moses had to be parted from his family and led into a different environment for his preparation. Samson was separated from the time of his birth. The disciples of Jesus, Nehemiah, Esther, Ruth, Joseph, and others were also separated from their communities.

When God prepares you, He won't necessarily explain why or for what purpose He is preparing you. After your preparation is complete, He will reveal the purpose behind it all.

God instructed Abraham to leave his country, relatives, and father's house. God couldn't bless him where he was. He needed to separate himself from those three aspects of his life before he could fulfill God's destiny. The Apostle Paul noted that he was set apart from birth for the calling he was engaged in (Galatians 1:15).

Throughout the Bible, you can see that God reveals His plans for people through dreams, parents, friends, relatives, and various other methods—like Mordecai, Joseph, John the Baptist, Samson, and Hannah, to name a few.

Even if you think God is a God of surprises, He prefers to disclose something before it happens—so He will receive the glory.

Esau was a man who sought immediate gratification. He gave up his long-term blessing for fleeting selfish pleasure.

God's plan is always multi-generational, not short-term. When God gives you an ability or revelation, it is not only for you to enjoy but also for someone else.

So, If you feel separated from your family and friends and feel like you are the strange fish in the pond or the strange sheep in the fold that doesn't look and behave like the others, know that you are in good company. If you fit in for the sake of feeling accepted by others, beware that you could miss out on what God has in store for you.

Preparation

Most of us make mistakes during this season of preparation, which I will explain as the Holy Spirit granted me the wisdom to do so.

In the next chapter, titled "Wilderness: God's School of Preparation," I explain this in detail.

Realization

After completing your preparation, God will reveal His true plan to you. The reason He doesn't tell you His plan earlier, is that if you knew what God was going to do with you, you would intentionally try to avoid troubles and face the struggles of life with a different attitude. You would neglect to trust God, and instead use your ability to overcome the obstacles.

However, if you don't know what He is preparing you for, you will learn to cling to Him when things don't go your way. He wants you to trust Him completely. Total surrender is His plan for your life.

At the burning bush, God revealed to Moses the exact purpose of the preparation he went through for the previous eighty long years. Moses understood God's plan that day. He thought it was all far too late.

Manifestation

Manifestation is the actual fulfillment of the purpose of God in your life. Everything that you ever dreamt about will come to pass one-by-one. Even more than you ever dreamt will happen in your life:[1]

> Now to Him who is able to do exceedingly abundantly above all that we ask or think, according to the power that works in us. Ephesians 3:20

WAIT FOR GOD'S TIMING

Many great men and women of God stumble when it comes to God's timing for their lives. Either they want to jump ahead, or, lag behind. Many people think that if God has spoken to them concerning their lives, all they need to do is just wait for God's timing.

---

1 As soon as God releases me into that level, I will be writing more about it.

It is God's complete responsibility to fulfill His word. However, if you do not take the initiative in the process, based on His guidance, it will always simply stay as just a good idea.

The Bible says it is impossible to please God without faith (Hebrews 11:6). If you go into God's presence, you need to go to Him with faith. Without works, your faith is dead (James 2:26).

Even the ants prepare their food for the winter during the summer, and trees prepare ahead of time for each season (Proverbs 30:25).

The first thing you should do when you receive a revelation from God about your life is to enter God's presence in order to understand His timing and direction for it.

It takes strict discipline to hear and follow God's voice. If God promised you something, it is for an appointed time. God promised Abraham a son, but Abraham couldn't understand nor ask Him for its timing.

Do not try to help God in bringing your dream to fulfillment by doing something in the flesh.

It was twenty-five years later that God fulfilled His word to Abraham. Likewise, God promised the Messiah, and it took four-thousand years. The Bible says that in the fullness of time, God sent his son born of a woman (Galatians 4:4). God promised Israel's return after seventy years in captivity (Jeremiah 29:10).

God is a God of timing. Everything under the sun has a season. Only in that season will it fully bloom. If you try to force it, you will lose much of it and experience the conflict in your household that Abraham faced. You will give birth to an *Ishmael* rather than an *Isaac*. The consequences of that disobedience are still evident among Jews and Muslims.

The Waiting Period

The waiting period is the hardest. Have you ever waited for someone who didn't show up on time, leaving you feeling upset?

Sometimes this is how we feel with God. We expect certain things, and when they don't happen on our schedule, we tend to act based on our own assumption or understanding. If you approach things this way, you will miss out in the long run.

Patience is a virtue that God requires of us. The Bible states that we inherit the promises through patience (Hebrews 6:12).

God told Noah it was going to rain. However, it didn't rain until he was 500 years old. Joseph had a dream about his life, but he didn't stand before Pharaoh until he was thirty years of age. Moses couldn't grasp God's timing for his life, so he tried to act as the deliverer before the appointed time. After waiting eighty years, he no longer wanted to carry out that role. The people of Israel were in Egypt for over 400 years, and then wandered in the wilderness for another forty years. God spoke that to Abraham hundreds of years before (Genesis 15:13). But it seemed Moses was not aware of it. Jesus came to fulfill God's plan, but He didn't start His ministry until He was thirty years old. The coming of the Lord will occur at the appointed time in your life.

KNOWING GOD'S DIRECTION

Once you know God's timing, you need God's direction. He has a specific plan of how you should go about fulfilling His plan for your life.

When Nehemiah learned about the suffering of his people, he didn't simply form a committee, head to Jerusalem, or start fundraising. He felt compelled to take action but was uncertain about how to proceed. Instead of quitting his job to attend a Bible college, he chose to fast and pray until he received guidance from the Lord, demonstrating his wisdom.

God provides direction in many ways. Sometimes, He sends people to confirm what He has already told you. However, it's important to listen to these messages very carefully, as people often add their own interpretations to what God has instructed them to say. This means there's a risk of being misled, as happened to Abraham. It might even be someone close to you presenting an idea that is hard to refuse. Remember the prophet who was deceived by another prophet and was killed by the lion (1 Kings 13:11-26)?

The Bible says that the thief comes to steal, kill, and destroy. The first thing the devil will try to do is to steal. What does he want to steal from you? He wants to steal your destiny, peace, joy, and prosperity; whatever God gave you, he wants to steal.

Jesus came to give life and to give it abundantly. He came to defeat the devil. 1 John 3:8 states that He came to destroy the works of the devil.

In Mark chapter five, we encounter a man whose destiny the devil sought to ruin. He was possessed by demons. No one wanted to associate with him; he lived in the wilderness and tombs. He had been cast out from his family, had no friends, and many may have said he wouldn't amount to anything in life.

The first place the devil attacks in your life, is your mind. If he can control the way you think, he can also control your life.

Your destiny attracts demons. How you fulfill your destiny depends on how you think about yourself and others. If you don't think the way God wants you to think, it becomes impossible to believe what God says about you.

This is why the Bible says to keep your heart with all diligence, for out of it flow the issues of life (Proverbs 4:23). When the Bible says heart, it usually means your mind.

The devil possesses more spiritual discernment than most Christians. He is more familiar with Bible verses than many ministers. He will attempt to subvert God's plan, just as he did in the beginning, by casting tempting thoughts your way.

The devil understands what God aims to achieve in your life. He is aware of the promises God has made to you. Even though the devil cannot read your mind, he can hear it as soon as you speak about your destiny.

The person in Mark chapter five was strong and powerful, mightier than many heavyweight champions. He couldn't be bound with fetters and chains; no man could tame him because of the demons inside him.

Many people are intelligent and strong, yet they lack true strength in the areas that matter most. He cried out for deliverance, but no one was there to help. He was desperate for assistance. Even though it was the demons who sought to kill him by cutting him with stones, he wished for death. The demons did everything they could to kill this man. I believe over six thousand worked together to thwart God's purpose for him—to prevent him from becoming a preacher and evangelist.

He thought Jesus was the one tormenting him:

> And he cried out with a loud voice and said, "What have I to do with You, Jesus, Son of the Most High God? I implore You by God that You do not torment me. Mark 5:7

How many believers today blame the evil that happens in their life, on God? Jesus came not to torment us, but to deliver us from the tormentor of our soul.

The interesting part of this story comes when Jesus commanded the demons to leave that man. The demons begged to enter a herd of swine, which then ran violently down a steep place into the sea and drowned.

From this, we understand that demons were trying all along to kill this man and destroy his destiny. When Jesus asked his name, he replied that it was *Legion*. There were at least 6,000 demons attempting to ruin the man. To destroy a person, is to destroy his destiny; however, because God had a plan for this man, the demons couldn't kill him.

Let me remind you that your purpose is greater than any demonic force out there or any government trying to prevent you from fulfilling what God wants you to do. That cannot happen. There are many examples of this in the Bible.

You may be a person like this man, without many friends and rejected by everyone you know; and not have many talents like other people do.

I remember the days when I cried out to God, asking for the purpose of my life and pleading with Him to explain why He created me. My dad told me I wouldn't be able to do anything because I was stupid and worthless.

I didn't have many friends. I often wondered what was wrong with me and why God created me without any talents or abilities. I felt this way because I was unaware of my purpose.

This man's family, society, and *church* rejected him, but one touch from God can make all the difference. Jesus cast out the demons out of this man. He wanted him to be a preacher declaring the mighty works of God.

He wanted to follow Jesus, but Jesus sent him out to tell his friends what the Lord had done for him. In Mark 5:20 we read that He began to publish in Decapolis the great things Jesus had done for him, and all the men marveled.

When God blesses you and transforms your life, you become a wonder to many (Psalm 71:7); and those who mocked you, will start seeking out your company. Those who disdain you today, will come to you for advice. Those who said you are worthless, will approach you to borrow from your blessings. Those who once avoided conversing with you, will begin to ask you questions about what transpired.

In John chapter nine, we read a similar story—about a blind man whose sight Jesus restored. I believe all the miracles Jesus performed had a strategic purpose. He didn't go around healing and delivering everyone He encountered, but rather just a select few. Jesus didn't resurrect all those who had died.

He was attracted by the purpose of those people the devil was trying to spoil. God is in the business of making straight all of the things that stand between you and your destiny.

There are thousands of testimonies around you of those who were messed up in their life, but whom God transformed through a miracle, to turn them around. And when they came to their right mind, they recognized what had happened.

Jesus came at the right moment to set this enslaved man free.

The people saw that this man was sitting and in his right mind, and they were afraid (Mark 5:15). I wonder why people were not afraid when he was a demoniac. Avoid associating with those who will kill your dreams or have a negative influence on you.

There are many people in this world who are not in their right minds, yet God has a destiny for their lives. Many of the future great evangelists are in tombs and in the wilderness, running and searching for someone to come and set them free.

Prayer

Prayer is not just an option; it is a necessity. Prayer plays a major role in fulfilling your purpose. It's like a hen brooding over her eggs, as prayer nurtures and shapes your dreams. Certain events in our lives occur through prayer that can only happen in that context. Prayer bridges the supernatural and the natural.

You have a significant role in fulfilling God's Word regarding your life. When you receive the promise, or after you identify your seed, you need to prepare for God to bring it to fruition.

Hannah needed a child, and she prayed and prayed until she made a commitment to God by giving Him the child before he was born (1 Samuel 1:10-11). She received her miracle.

Daniel prayed for the release of his people from captivity even though it had been seventy years. His prayer played a major role in fulfilling God's Word, which He prophesied through Jeremiah many years before.

The Messiah was promised, but it was not until two individuals fully dedicated their lives to seeing it fulfilled that it came to pass. They were Anna and Simeon. The Bible states that if any two agree on earth and ask Him for anything in His name, He will do it for us (Matthew 18:19). In this case, two were agreeing in spirit for one reason: God had promised Simeon that he wouldn't die until he saw the Messiah with his own eyes.

Jesus promised that the Holy Spirit would be present after He ascended to heaven. However, it wasn't until the hundred and twenty disciples waited for ten days in prayer that He arrived (Acts 2:1-4).

Nineveh was not going to be saved until Jonah was going to preach there.

You may sometimes think that if God wanted to accomplish something, He would find someone for the task. No. He has a specific person designated for each job. No one else can do what you can do. No one else will be able to achieve what Moses did.

It was only after the church fasted and prayed that the Holy Spirit instructed them to send out Paul and Barnabas to preach the Gospel. Therefore, we received the Gospel

Haman planned to kill all the Jews, including Mordecai, but Esther and all the Jews fasted and prayed for three days, and God intervened in their lives.

No, God's will for you is not to perish and live a miserable life in bondage.

The people were in bondage, and not until they cried out to God did He send Moses to deliver them. If they had not cried out, they would have remained in captivity for many more years.

You will never see your dream or purpose fulfilled until you initiate it under God's guidance, as described above.

CHAPTER 11

The Wilderness – God's School of Preparation

After God separates us for His purpose, He starts to prepare us for the task ahead. Only those who pass through this preparation successfully will receive the anointing and the wealth of God to fulfill their destiny on this earth.

We simply need patience and perseverance, as preparation is a slow and steady process that cannot be completed in just one day. We cannot speed up the process. It is similar to the growth of a baby in the womb.

By preparing successfully, you will receive the anointing and wealth of God to fulfill your destiny on this earth.

If you resist Him in the preparation, it can go on longer than intended. God is long-suffering and abundant in mercy, so He will keep giving you chances until you die.

OUR GOD IS A GOD OF ORDER

Whatever He creates or does, has an order. When you break His order, you end up in chaos, whether in your family life, church life, or in your walk with Him. When you break the order, it causes pain, and you lose more than you need to.

When you examine the life of the Israelites, you discover the outcomes of this powerful principle. Their history is well-documented in the Bible for our example and guidance.

When they came out of Egypt, God didn't take them straight to the Promised Land—their spiritual inheritance. Instead, He took them into the wilderness. After completing the wilderness experience, they still had to cross the river Jordan.

The Wilderness Experience

The experience involved a three-part training process that God appointed for them before they could enjoy their blessing. The time they spent between their exodus from Egypt and their crossing of the Jordan River is referred to as the wilderness experience.

The period from the moment you were born again until you begin walking in the destiny that God has ordained for you is called your wilderness experience. The wilderness serves as God's order and training period, where He equips you to become who He intends you to be.

If you try to go past the wilderness and try to enter your spiritual inheritance—your destiny—you will end up as prey to your enemies.

Wilderness Duration

The duration of the wilderness experience varies from person to person. Joseph spent thirteen years in the wilderness, while Moses spent forty years there; it was during this time before he became Deliverer that God appeared to him in the burning bush on Mount Horeb at the age of 80, calling him to return to Egypt and lead the Israelites out of slavery (Exodus chapter three).

Abraham waited many years for the fulfillment of God's promise to give him descendants and the land of Canaan. Twenty-five years passed between the time God promised Abraham a son and the birth of Isaac. Abraham was 75 years old when the promise was made and 100 years old when Isaac was born (Genesis 12:4; Genesis 21:5). The Spirit led Jesus into the wilderness after He was baptized and filled with the Holy Spirit. The Apostle Paul spent fourteen years in the desert of Arabia.

Unfortunately, most of the Israelites who left Egypt never entered their spiritual inheritance. Sadly, many today wander in their own wilderness, living a mediocre life.

For you, the wilderness is not a geographical location like it was in the Old Testament; rather, it is a season in your life during which God shapes your character and refines your attitudes and motivation.

The table below explains the sequence of how this process worked in the Old Testament and in our lives as New Covenant believers.

Egypt	Red Sea	Wilder-ness	Jordan	Enemies	Promised Land
Salva-tion	Baptism	Wilder-ness	Dying to self	Devil	Divine Destiny

Sin	Flesh	Dying to self	Baptism of the Holy Spirit	Devil	Inher-itance
Called		Chosen		Faithful	

In the Christian world, we don't typically teach the order presented in the chart above; instead, it often appears to be reversed, resembling something like the example below.

After a person gets saved, they are often warned only about the devil, while little is said about the flesh. They typically receive no teaching on how to keep the devil away and overcome their fleshly desires, or how to enforce his defeat when they are ready. Rarely are they taught what is necessary to resist the devil, conquer their fleshly desires, and eventually enforce his defeat when the right time comes.

Devil————————Sin————————Inheritance

Each experience the Israelites went through, teaches a powerful lesson that is essential if you are serious about fulfilling God's purpose for your life. God included these events to demonstrate His order. This will reveal how you can enjoy your salvation and receive all that God has in store for you.

If you disobey His order, you will find yourself in a mess. In Egypt, the Israelites didn't fight to free themselves from bondage. God fought the battle for them. All they had to do was believe the Word of the Lord and pack their belongings. Forgiveness of sin is free in Christ. You don't have to fight to be saved; you simply accept the free gift:

> For by grace you have been saved through faith, and that not of yourselves; it is the gift of God, not of works, lest anyone should boast. Ephesians 2:8-9

Moses, who symbolizes Jesus in the Old Testament, confronted the Egyptian Pharaoh—who represents the devil in our context. Egypt signifies the bondage of sin.

The Israelites had nothing to lose. They were instructed to slaughter a lamb and apply its blood to their doorposts. That lamb represented Jesus Christ—the Lamb of God who takes away the sins of the world (John 1:29). It was an act of faith. You also receive your salvation by faith.

Once God brought them out of Egypt, they were God's property. God appointed the cloud by day and fire by night to protect them. He appointed His Angel to guide them (Exodus 23:20). When their enemy tried to pursue them and overtake them, He did the battle for them. He didn't let the Egyptians come near them.

This is a vivid reminder of how God defends what is His, surrounding His people with His presence and waging war against those threatening them. Isn't this an incredible testimony to His power and love?

Once you are saved by His grace, you are God's property, and no one can touch you. It doesn't matter how powerful the enemy is or what kind of threat he is. You are safe if God is on your side (Romans 8:31).

God didn't tell them to fear Pharaoh when they came out of Egypt. The Bible says in John 10:28-29: "And I give them eternal life, and they shall never perish; neither shall anyone snatch them out of My hand. My Father, who has given them to Me, is greater than all; and no one is able to snatch them out of My Father's hand."

You may say, if God was so concerned about them, why did they run out of water during the first week?

This is how God trains us: He wants us to trust in Him for our daily needs. They didn't have any food to eat, and God wanted them to understand that man does not live by bread alone, but by His Word.

To the natural mind, this may sound crazy. However, God's ways are higher than our ways, and His thoughts are higher than our thoughts. He wants to keep things simple for us, but we keep trying to complicate it—often making things more complicated by trying to help Him out.

Many Misunderstand God's Divine Order

Once people get saved, they often believe they are ready to march straight into the Promised Land and defeat the enemy. No, please don't make that mistake—you will end up overpowered by the enemy, and deeply regret it.

To inherit your spiritual inheritance in the Kingdom of God, you must first successfully come out of the wilderness. Many people attend church because someone told them that salvation would bring blessings and solve all their problems.

They get saved and continue for a while. When God starts to address their flesh, they feel uncomfortable and run out the back door. No one told them, that in order to inherit the blessings, they need to overcome their flesh. As a result, people get saved and continue for a while.

When they see that what they were promised is not coming to them, they become offended, exit the church, and talk disparagingly about God and His people. Ultimately, they inflict more damage on the Body of Christ and bring disgrace to His name among the heathen.

God guides you into the wilderness in order to prepare you for crossing the Jordan river—which symbolizes dying to self or overcoming the flesh.

Some believe that once they are saved, all that awaits them on this earth is misery and sadness until they die and enter their

Promised Land in Heaven. Others do not accept that we have an inheritance on this earth, thinking instead that their entire inheritance is reserved for Heaven.

After entering the Promised Land, the Israelites had to fight and kill the inhabitants. If our inheritance is only in Heaven who are we going to fight after we die? After we pass from this earth, we don't go to fight any enemy; we wait for the Judgment Day. After entering the Promised Land, the Israelites had to confront and eliminate the inhabitants.

The Bible states that our last enemy is death; it is appointed for man to die once, and then face the judgment (Hebrews 9:27).

Let's wake up, shake off all feeble theologies, put on the full armor of God, and prepare to claim our inheritance.

Matthew 5:5 says: *"Blessed are the meek: for they shall inherit the earth."* (KJV)

Which earth are you going to inherit?

If you are going to leave the earth, and go somewhere, when do you inherit the earth? Psalm 37:9 says: "… But those that wait upon the LORD, they shall inherit the earth." (KJV)

We see in our churches today that many are wandering about in the wilderness. They don't know why God brought them out to the wilderness. They think it is the devil that is causing them to experience all the struggles, because that is what they hear from most preachers.

So, they begin to call up fights with the devil, only to see that the more they fight, the more battles increase.

The Israelites themselves didn't understand the purpose either, which led them to murmur and complain until they perished in the wilderness without seeing the Promised Land. It was not the devil who caused shortages of water in wilderness.

The first problem they experienced was thirst. It was more than a thirst for water.

God brought you into the wilderness to teach you how to bring your flesh under control. After you overcome sin and receive forgiveness, the next step is to deal with the flesh. If you go to battle before taking care of the flesh, you invite the devil to bring unnecessary troubles.

Your victory over sin won't last long unless your flesh is brought under subjection.

Once you know your life's purpose—the seed that God has planted in your spirit—you need to let everything in you die that is not pleasing to the Lord. The seed has to die before it changes its form and becomes a plant.

God deals with your flesh because no flesh shall glory in His presence (Romans 8:8). Why does God hate the flesh and its works so much?

God cannot stand before sin. He hates sin but loves the sinner. Sin brought the works of the flesh into your life.

We have many wounded Christians who went to fight to possess their inheritance before they were ready. They remain ineffective and always have a horror story to tell about the devil.

There is nothing worse than facing the devil with human strength and understanding. The devil is not afraid of screaming or shouting if there is no spiritual wisdom behind the shout and screams.

You don't conquer the devil through your own strength but by spiritual wisdom. The wilderness experience imparts this wisdom. Even our Lord Jesus had to learn obedience through the trials He faced.

Hebrews 5:8 says: **"Though He were a Son,** yet He learned obedience by the things which He suffered." (KJV)

Ecclesiastes 9:13-15 says: "This wisdom I have also seen under the sun, and it seemed great to me: There was a little city with few men in it; and a great king came against it, besieged it, and built great snares around it. Now there was found in it a poor wise man, and he by his wisdom delivered the city. Yet no one remembered that same poor man."

Many are called but few are chosen (**Matthew 22:14**).

Everyone who left Egypt received the call. However, they had to endure the trials of the wilderness in order to be chosen. Once selected, and upon entering the Promised Land, they had to remain faithful until the end in order to receive their earthly inheritance.

If you are saved, you are called. However, whether God will entrust you with His treasure to fulfill that call depends on how you emerge from your wilderness training.

When the Israelites reached the wilderness, the first battle they encountered was with the Amalekites. They didn't initiate the fight; instead, the Amalekites came out to battle the Israelites.

Who are these Amalekites? Why didn't the Philistines or others come to fight? What do they symbolize?

If you study about the Amalekites in scripture (Exodus 17:8), you will see that they are the descendants of Esau, the brother of Jacob. Esau was the man who sold his spiritual inheritance for the momentary gratification of his flesh. He traded his birthright for a bowl of stew.

After that incident, he does not show any signs of repentance. Instead, he chose a lifestyle that was contrary to his father Isaac. That is how Abraham's grandson became the leader of heathen nations. He became the father of the Edomites.

In Genesis 36:1-12, you read about Esau's generations: Esau had a son named Eliphaz, and Amalek was Eliphaz's son.

The Amalekites are the people who live by the flesh and its desires and have nothing to do with spiritual inheritance. For them, fleshly gratification was more important than spiritual inheritance.

Every time you react in the flesh to satisfy its desires, you miss out on your spiritual inheritance. This is why the Bible says those who live according to the flesh cannot please God (Romans 8:8).

The first enemy you face in the wilderness is not the devil, but your flesh.

The Israelites lacked water, which is a basic physical necessity. In their natural state, they reacted instead of trusting God to provide for them.

Whenever you respond from the flesh to a spiritual issue, you miss out on the blessings that God has in store for you.

Rather than trusting that the One Who called them out could provide for them, they complained and rebelled against God and Moses.

If you don't conquer the flesh in the wilderness, you won't be able to defeat the enemies in your Promised Land.

Knowing Whether you Have Passed the Wilderness Test?

How do you know whether you have passed the Wilderness test? Have you murmured lately? Do you wish those who aggravate and hate you would just drop dead? Can you trust God during times of scarcity? Do you lose your temper when faced with stress and pressure? Have you spoken against your spiritual authorities recently? Have you stepped outside of God's timing and acted out of impatience? Are you able to walk by faith rather than by sight? Do you need to see or feel something before you believe it? Do you sometimes feel very close to God, while at other times, you question whether you are even saved?

Your responses to the questions above will reveal how many more mountains you need to navigate before crossing the Jordan River and entering your Promised Land of inheritance.

Before Moses sent Joshua to battle the Amalekites, he needed to prepare Joshua to conquer his own flesh, before he could entrust him with leadership of His people. Moses ascended the mountain to pray for Joshua.

Your Victory Over your Flesh is Directly Connected to your Prayer Life

The number one weapon to overcome your flesh is prayer. Prayer combined with fasting will bring tremendous victory over your flesh.

Jesus said: "... Pray that you enter not into temptation" Luke 22:40.

The devil brings temptations. The works of the flesh lure you to give in to temptation, but when you pray, your flesh is placed under the control of your spirit, and you gain victory over such temptations.

Exodus 17:11 states, "And it came to pass, when Moses held up his hands, that Israel prevailed: and when he let down his hands, Amalek prevailed."

Isn't that interesting? As long as prayer is present, your flesh will remain subdued; but when you lack a disciplined prayer life, your fleshly desires grow stronger. The only way to overcome temptation, is to overcome your flesh; the only way to overcome the flesh, is prayer.

When Joshua defeated the Amalekites, Moses built an altar there and named it "Jehovah-Nissi," which means 'The Lord Is My Banner.' Exodus 17:16 says; *"For he said, because the LORD hath sworn that the LORD will have war with Amalek from generation to generation."* (KJV)

The war with the Amalekites did not end there; it continued from one generation to the next. God's principles remain consistent across generations because His Word does not change.

Why the Majority Couldn't Enter the Promised Land

We will examine the scriptures to discover why most people were unable to enter the Promised Land. Was it the devil or the flesh?

We are going to read from 1 Corinthians 10:1-11, which shows the real reasons why Israel perished in the wilderness:

> Moreover, brethren, I do not want you to be unaware that all our fathers were under the cloud, all passed through the sea, all were baptized into Moses in the cloud and in the sea, all ate the same spiritual food, and all drank the same spiritual drink.
>
> For they drank of that spiritual Rock that followed them, and that Rock was Christ. But with most of them God was not well pleased, for their bodies were scattered in the wilderness.
>
> Now these things became our examples, to the intent that we should not lust after evil things as they also lusted. And do not become idolaters as were some of them.

As it is written, "The people sat down to eat and drink, and rose up to play." Nor let us commit sexual immorality, as some of them did, and in one day twenty-three thousand fell; nor let us tempt Christ, as some of them also tempted, and were destroyed by serpents; nor complain, as some of them also complained, and were destroyed by the destroyer.

Now all these things happened to them as examples, and they were written for our admonition, upon whom the ends of the ages have come.

Dear saints of God, do you see what I see?

In the passage above, I don't see the Holy Spirit saying they perished in the wilderness because of the devil. The children of Israel perished in the wilderness not from fighting against the devil or other nations, but rather from fighting against themselves:

Fools, because of their transgression, and because of their iniquities, were afflicted. Psalm 107:17

They were their own enemies. God had no choice but to destroy them because if they couldn't conquer their own weaknesses, how could they hope to defeat the enemies waiting for them in the Promised Land?

If you cannot control your passions, forget about overcoming the devil. They didn't perish because they were unable to defeat the principality.

Who was the intended audience of the Apostle Paul's message in 1 Corinthians 10:1-11? It was directed not to the heathen but to the believers in Corinth.

About whom did he write?

The Apostle Paul was writing not about some heathen nation. This is about God's own people—whom He redeemed by His own mighty hand.

The first four verses of 1 Corinthians 10:1- 4 reveal the kind of people the Apostle Paul is referring to:

1. **They were our fathers (verse 1)**

2. **They were under the cloud—God's glory (verse 1)**

3. **They passed through the Red Sea—God delivered them from the enemy of their soul (verse 1)**

4. **They were all baptized—leaving their sin behind (verse 2)**

5. **They all ate the spiritual meal, bread from heaven— Communion (verse 3)**

6. **They all drank the spiritual drink—Communion (verse 4)**

7. **They drank from the spiritual Rock—Christ (verse 4)**

What went wrong with these wonderful people?

The problem wasn't due to any failure on God's part.

The Bible tells us that we must learn from their example so that we won't repeat the same things.

Mistakes you can learn from

What were some of the characteristics and mistakes these people made?

1. **God was not pleased with them (verse 5)**

2. **God overthrew them in the wilderness (verse 5)**

3. They lusted after evil things (verse 2)

4. They were idolaters (verse 2)

5. They were drunkards (verse 2)

6. They committed fornication (verse 2)

7. They tempted Christ (verse 2)

8. They murmured against their leadership and against God (verse 10).

All the above actions were not caused by the devil, rather they are the works of the flesh (Mark 7:20-23).

The Bible states in Galatians 5:21, that those who live according to the flesh shall not inherit the kingdom of God.

If you want to enjoy the blessings of the kingdom, you need to overcome the flesh.

If you closely examine each manifestation of the flesh listed in Galatians 5:19-20 against the lives of the Israelites in the wilderness, you'll find they stumbled in each of those areas at one time or another.

Works of the flesh

We are going to explore the works of the flesh mentioned below, and how the Israelites encountered these eighteen in their lives:

1) Adultery

Numbers 25:1 (KJV) says: "And Israel abode in Shittim, and the people began to commit whoredom with the daughters of Moab." If you study the golden calf incident, there are a few of these works of the flesh which manifested in that one incident.

2) Fornication

1 Corinthians 10:8 (KJV) warns us: "Nor let us commit sexual immorality, as some of them did, and in one day twenty-three thousand fell;"

3) Uncleanness

Psalm 106:28 & 39 (KJV) says: "They joined themselves unto Baalpeor, and ate the sacrifices of the dead. Thus they defiled with their own works, and went a whoring with their own inventions."

4) Lasciviousness

Psalm 106:14 (KJV) says: "But lusted exceedingly in the wilderness, and tempted God in the desert."

5) Idolatry

When they saw Moses delayed from coming down from the mountain, they asked Aaron to make a god to lead them in their journey; and he made the golden calf.

Psalm 106:19-20 says: "They made a calf in Horeb, and worshipped the molten image. Thus they changed their glory into the similitude of an ox that eateth grass"

1 Corinthians 10:7 (KJV) warns: "Neither be ye idolaters, as were some of them, as it is written, the people sat down to eat and drink, and rose up to play."

6) Witchcraft

1 Samuel 15:23 says: "For rebellion is as the sin of witchcraft, and stubbornness is as iniquity and idolatry ..."

Psalm 107: 11-12 says, "Because they rebelled against the words of God, and condemned the counsel of the most high. Therefore

He brought down their heart with labour; they fell down, and there was none to help."

We know more than anything that they rebelled against God and Moses more than any other sins.

7) Hatred

They hated Moses' leadership and God's promises:

"Yea, they despised the pleasant land, they believed not his word. But murmured in their tents, and hearkened not unto the voice of the LORD" (Psalm 106:24-25 KJV).

8) Variance (difference of opinion)

When the twelve spies came back from spying out the land they brought a difference of opinion.

Numbers 13:30-31 (KJV) says: "And Caleb stilled the people before Moses, and said, Let us go up at once, and possess it; for we are well able to overcome it. But the men that went up with him said, we be not able to go up against the people; for they are stronger than we."

10) Emulations (Selfish ambitions)

Numbers 12:1-2 (KJV) says: "And Miriam and Aaron spake against Moses because of the Ethiopian woman whom he had married: for he had married an Ethiopian woman. And they said, hath the LORD indeed spoken only by Moses? Hath he not spoken also by us? And the LORD heard it."

11) Wrath

Numbers 16:1-22 (KJV). Verse 15 says: "And Moses was very wroth, and said unto the LORD, respect not thou their offering; I have not taken one ass from them, neither have I hurt one of them."

12) Strife

Psalm 106:32 (KJV) says: "They angered Him also at the waters of strife, so that it went ill with Moses on account of them;"

13) Seditions (Speech that causes rebellion)

Numbers 16:1-3 (KJV) says: "Now Korah, the son of Izhar, the son of Kohath, the son of Levi, and Dathan and Abiram, the sons of Eliab, and On, the son of Peleth, sons of Reuben, took men:

And they rose up before Moses, with certain of the children of Israel, two hundred and fifty princes of the assembly, famous in the congregation, men of renown: And they gathered themselves together against Moses and against Aaron, and said unto them, Ye take too much upon you, seeing all the congregation are holy, every one of them, and the Lord is among them: wherefore then lift ye up yourselves above the congregation of the Lord?"

14). Heresies (contradicting doctrine)

1 Corinthians 10:10 (KJV) says: "Neither murmur ye, as some of them also murmured, and were destroyed of the destroyer."

All the conflicting doctrines in the church are the direct result of the flesh. When all the believers overcome their flesh, there will be only one church and one denomination.

15) Envying

Psalm 106:16 (KJV) says: "They envied Moses also in the camp, and Aaron the saint of the Lord."

16) Murders

Psalm 106:37-38 (KJV) says: "Yea, they sacrificed their sons and their daughters unto devils. And shed innocent blood, even the blood of their sons and daughters, whom they sacrificed unto the idols of Canaan: and the land was polluted with blood."

17) Drunkenness

Exodus 32:6 (KJV) says: "And they rose up early in the morrow, and offered burnt offerings and brought peace offerings; and the people sat down to eat and to drink, and rose up to play."

18) Reveling (riotous partying)

Exodus 32:6 (KJV) says: "And they rose up early in the morrow, and offered burnt offerings and brought peace offerings; and the people sat down to eat and to drink, and rose up to play."

The Bible says that if you do any of the above, you will not inherit the kingdom of God.

Do you know why not all Christians receive the same amount of blessings, even though God loves us all equally? If you wish to enjoy the blessings of the kingdom, you need to overcome the flesh.

Jesus came to offer abundant life, and it is for everyone. The phrase "inherit the kingdom" in Galatians 5:21 means while you are here on earth, you won't inherit the riches and abundant life that Jesus promised.

Many mighty men and women who had a powerful call on their lives perished in the wilderness because they couldn't overcome their flesh. Even today, many talented people who have great potential wander in the wilderness, struggling with secret sins.

King Saul was a remarkable figure with immense potential, but he lost the battle against the Amalekites, and was ultimately killed by an Amalekite while fighting the Philistines.

The Bible says in 1 Samuel 9:2, "And he had a choice and handsome son whose name was Saul. There was not a more handsome person than he among the children of Israel. From his shoulders upward he was taller than any of the people."

All the physical qualities mentioned above didn't make Saul a great king. He couldn't keep his flesh under control. Although he was anointed and even prophesied a few times.

In 1 Samuel 10:8, we read that Samuel instructed Saul to wait seven days for him to join him to offer peace offerings. In 1 Samuel 13:8, we learn that Saul waited for six days, but on the seventh day, he grew impatient and could no longer wait. He decided to take on the role of the priest and proceeded to offer the sacrifices. As soon as he finished, the Prophet Samuel arrived.

1 Samuel 13:13 says: "And Samuel said to Saul, "You have done foolishly. You have not kept the commandment of the Lord your God, which He commanded you. For now the Lord would have established your kingdom over Israel forever." God had a plan to establish the kingdom of Saul and his descendants forever in Israel.

God is a merciful God and the God of second chances. He gave one more chance for Saul to prove that he could keep his flesh conquered. The Bible says: "He who is slow to anger is better than the mighty, and he who rules his spirit than he who takes a city." (Proverbs 16:32).

1 Samuel 15:1-3 says:

> Samuel also said to Saul, "The Lord sent me to anoint you king over His people, over Israel. Now therefore, heed the voice of the words of the Lord. Thus says the Lord of hosts:
>
> 'I will punish Amalek for what he did to Israel, how he ambushed him on the way when he came up from

Egypt. Now go and attack Amalek, and utterly destroy all that they have, and do not spare them. But kill both man and woman, infant and nursing child, ox and sheep, camel and donkey.'"

However, when he saw them, Saul couldn't kill all the fat animals. Instead, he disobeyed God and lost his kingdom for some worthless animals. For him, those animals were more important than obeying God.

Do you keep anything in your life more important than God?

Where you spend most of your time shows where your heart is. Is it your own body, the TV, your house, friends, sport, food, or something else? I have seen people who, even while they pray, feel the need to nibble something or take a sip of coffee. No wonder they are still wandering around the same mountain for more than forty years.

In 2 Samuel 1:1-12 (KJV), we read about how Saul had died. Verse 8-10 says, "......And he said unto me, who art thou? And I answered him; I am an Amalekite. He said unto me again, Stand, I pray thee, upon me, and slay me: for anguish is come upon me, because my life is yet whole in me. So I stood upon him, and slew him ..."

This narrative follows the earlier account in 1 Samuel 15:3, where God commands Saul to annihilate the Amalekites. However, Saul disobeys by sparing their king, Agag, and keeping some of the livestock. The irony lies in the fact that an Amalekite—a member of the group Saul was supposed to destroy completely—later killed Saul. This reflects the consequences of Saul's incomplete obedience.

We read in 1 Peter 2:11: "Beloved, I beg you as sojourners and pilgrims, abstain from fleshly lusts which war against the soul," The fleshly lusts wage war against your soul to keep you defeated.

James 4:1 says: "Where do wars and fights come from among you? Do they not come from your desires for pleasure that war in your members?"

What will you do with these fleshly lusts which are symbolized by the Amalekites?

Deuteronomy 25: 17-19 says: "Remember what Amalek did to you on the way as you were coming out of Egypt, how he met you on the way and attacked your rear ranks, all the stragglers at your rear, when you were tired and weary; and he did not fear God. Therefore it shall be, when the Lord your God has given you rest from your enemies all around, in the land which the Lord your God is giving you to possess as an inheritance, that you will blot out the remembrance of Amalek from under heaven. You shall not forget."

If you don't take the works of the flesh seriously and address them, they will eventually catch up with you and destroy your destiny.

CHAPTER 12

The Purpose of Wilderness

TO DEVELOP GODLY CHARACTER

No parent chastises their mature child. Similarly, you correct your children when they are still young. God disciplines us when we are spiritually immature, because He wants us to grow in character.

The Bible states that God disciplines those He loves and instructs us not to rebel against His discipline. The wilderness experience is how God refines us.

Deuteronomy 8:5 says: "You should know in your heart that as a man chastens his son, so the Lord your God chastens you."

How does He discipline you? He guides you through experiences that you may not enjoy, which refine your attitudes and emotional stability to align with His Spirit. His goal is to cultivate the fruit of the Spirit within you.

If God is to trust you with His spiritual treasure, you must possess certain spiritual qualities. The Bible states in Ephesians 1:3: "Blessed be the God and Father of our Lord Jesus Christ, who has blessed us with every spiritual blessing in the heavenly places in Christ."

WHY THE WILDERNESS?

I believe there are two main reasons why God allows us to go through the wilderness. The first is to teach us humility.

Learning Humility

Deuteronomy 8:2-5 says: "And you shall remember that the Lord your God led you all the way these forty years in the wilderness, to humble you and test you, to know what was in your heart, whether you would keep His commandments or not.

So He humbled you, allowed you to hunger, and fed you with manna which you did not know nor did your fathers know, that He might make you know that man shall not live by bread alone; but man lives by every word that proceeds from the mouth of the Lord.

Your garments did not wear out on you, nor did your foot swell these forty years.

You should know in your heart that as a man chastens his son, so the Lord your God chastens you."

One of the powerful lessons we learn from the incarnation of Christ is how He came down to fight the devil. He didn't arrive as an arrogant tyrant ready to destroy the enemy's camps with mortars and shells. Instead, He embodied the opposite of what everyone imagined a king to be. He came to win a spiritual battle.

He came as a Humble Servant

First, what you need for the spiritual battle is humility. Christ laid aside all His heavenly glory and majesty and took on the form of a servant (Philippians 2:7). Many enter the fight with the pride and arrogance of their race, wealth, and intelligence. As a result, they get defeated and torn apart by the enemy.

The Bible teaches us to have the same mindset that Christ had while He was on this earth. The key to Jesus' victory over the devil was His humility, not His power. After all, power without humility is like fire in the hands of a three-year-old. Lord, teach us to be humble.

This is why you may feel irritated with others while going through your wilderness training. God is trying to address your pride and ego. He will often let you work with people you would rather avoid—especially those who know how to push your buttons.

He will take you to places you don't want to go. In the wilderness, everything is out in the open—no privacy and no secrets. Everyone wears the same clothes and shoes. You will have to learn to appreciate those people you don't naturally get along with in the flesh.

Additionally, you must accept them and show them the love of God. When you can do this, you are ready for something big. Deuteronomy 8:16 says: "who fed you in the wilderness with manna, which your fathers did not know, that He might humble you and that He might test you, to do you good in the end—"

Learning Patience

Secondly, God leads you into wilderness training to teach you patience. For some people, just hearing that word, immediately irritates them.

A friend from Bible School and I used to call ourselves "long-distance friends" even though we lived in the same building. This was because we had opposite temperaments and couldn't get close without making each other uncomfortable and angry.

How many people might have accomplished great things in their lives if they had more patience?

The Bible says in Hebrews 6:12: "Who fed you in the wilderness with manna, which your fathers did not know, that He might humble you and that He might test you, to do you good in the end—"

How does God develop patience in you?

He does so by requiring you to repeat the same thing again and again. At other times, He develops patience by teaching you to wait for His timing.

The Israelites didn't have very many choices in the wilderness. They had the same food, water, and people around them all the time. Can you imagine that for forty years? Yet, they still failed and didn't allow God to develop their patience.

Do you sometimes wish you had just disappeared and not had to deal with your situation? Wait a minute—perhaps God is trying to build you up.

I felt that many times in my life. I didn't know what I was going through was meant to develop me. I thought it was the devil trying to mess with me. I didn't have anyone to guide me or anyone I could approach with such questions.

This is why God led me to write this book—to explain why you are going through what you are going through.

Faith and patience always go together. If you want faith, you need to be patient. If you need to be patient, you need faith. Hebrews 10:36 says: "For you have need of endurance, so that after you have done the will of God, you may receive the promise:"

You need patience if you need to receive what God has promised you.

One of the things that I learned about spiritual life is that what we gain through days of fasting, praying, and walking with the Lord can be blown apart by a minute of anger or impatience. Patience is a fruit of the spirit. The flesh cannot be patient because it is just the opposite of patience.

Do you want to discover how mature you are in spirit?

If you wish to emerge from the wilderness victorious, you need to cultivate the habit of doing the right things, even if you don't feel like doing them.

If you can pray when you don't feel like it, you are ready for a promotion. If you can read and meditate on the Word amidst stressful circumstances, your spirit is stronger than your flesh. When things go wrong, or when you get sick, if you turn to God first before seeking any other help, you are growing spiritually mature in the matters of God.

GET FAMILIAR WITH THE WORD OF GOD

This is how you successfully come out of your wilderness.

God's principles are eternal; they do not change with the times we are living in. You can have complete confidence in His unchanging nature and His eternal principles.

God Gave them Manna to Eat in the Wilderness

The first thing they said when they saw manna was, "What is this?" They didn't say, "Wow, what a nice-looking cake, can I have some?" Manna was the bread from heaven, symbolizing the Word of God.

They had to eat manna not just for breakfast, but also for lunch and dinner. They needed to collect it in the morning before sunrise. Why did God require this? Wasn't it tiring? Yes, it was. The reason was that God wanted them to become familiar with the bread from heaven.

The only exciting aspect of manna was that they received it fresh from heaven every day, even though it remained the same. God was preparing them to embrace the Word of God when they arrived at the Promised Land. He wanted them to meditate on His laws both day and night.

The Word of God is the most important thing you need to become familiar with while you are in the wilderness. It may not feel exciting at first.

I have heard people ask the same question the Israelites posed about manna when they begin to read the Word. You encounter the same Word each day, consistently, day in and day out. When you allow God to take priority in your life, He has something fresh to speak to you about daily from that same Word.

It may not look appealing, and you might not feel hungry, but you know it is heavenly, and it is God's Word. You might think you know all the Bible stories and ask, 'What else is there to know?'

Let me tell you, no one has even begun to explore the depth of wisdom hidden in those stories. Depending on what you're experiencing, those same stories will reveal something new that speaks to your situation.

Seek God First at the Beginning of a Day

The Israelites had to gather the manna early in the morning. If they waited and said they would sleep in for a while, they missed their food for the whole day. Even if they cried and complained, they had to go starving for that day. What a loss!

I don't know how many blessings I may have missed by not starting my day with God.

The Israelites had to collect only what they needed. One person could not do that for another.

If you study the life of David. he had the habit of seeking God early in the morning. Just look up in a concordance for the words "early" and "morning" in the book of Psalms and you will be surprised to see David's heart cry.

I want to write three scriptures here for you:

Psalm 63:1 says: "O God, You are my God; early will I seek You; my soul thirsts for You; my flesh longs for You in a dry and thirsty land where there is no water."

David sought God early in the morning, not because he was in the most comfortable place, but quite the opposite; he was in a land of no water, a land that was dry and thirsty.

Psalm 119:148 says: "My eyes are awake through the night watches, That I may meditate on Your word."

Psalm 130:5 & 6 says: I wait for the Lord, my soul waits, and in His word I do hope. My soul waits for the Lord more than those who watch for the morning—Yes, more than those who watch for the morning."

Listen to and Obey your Spiritual Authority

Pride can cause significant harm to others and yourself, often more than you realize. In the wilderness, the Israelites struggled to listen to Moses.

Your spiritual authority includes your pastor, your husband, and anyone God sends to help you grow spiritually.

At one point, Aaron and Miriam believed they could perform the same tasks as Moses. They were aware of the consequences of their actions. The Bible states that Moses had to intercede in order to spare Aaron's life; otherwise, God was ready to take him out (Deuteronomy 9:20).

Moses could have allowed God to destroy all the people. However, he was so meek and humble that he chose to intercede for them.

Thank God for leaders like these. However, there aren't many around today. Therefore, be cautious about your words and actions toward those who hold spiritual authority over you.

Hebrews 12:17 (KJV) says: "Obey them that have the rule over you, and submit yourselves: for they watch over your souls, as they that must give account, that they may do it with joy, and not with grief: that is unprofitable for you."

Galatians 6:6 (Amplified Bible) says, "Let him who receives instruction in the Word share all good things with his teacher (contributing to his support)."

Cross the River Jordan

Crossing the Jordan was a unique experience for the people of Israel, signifying a paradigm shift after forty years. They were approaching the end of their wanderings in the wilderness.

During their time in the wilderness, they marched under the cloud by day and the fire by night. There was something supernatural to guide them, requiring little faith. They could see the presence of God with their natural eyes. They walked by sight, not by faith.

God provided their daily food every morning, relieving them of worries about what to eat. The Rock, from which they drank water, followed them.

While in the wilderness, God worked in their flesh, not their spirits. He knew that they had to conquer their flesh before they could exercise their spirit to successfully move forward.

They recalled how God had parted the Red Sea when Moses stretched out the rod.

Now, Moses had died, and it would not be through their new leader, Joshua, that the Jordan would part. Joshua did not possess a rod like Moses did, and the cloud was absent to guide them.

Once they crossed over Jordan, visible supernatural signs would cease. They would no longer receive free food every morning, but they need not worry about what they would drink, as the Rock following them would not provide water.

Joshua instructed them to prepare food before they crossed over.

They could not complain or murmur once they crossed over (1 Corinthians 10:10). There is no indication that they complained or murmured against Joshua after they crossed Jordan.

CHANGE OF MINDSET

It was a change of government. It was a change of mindset. They had to look at the Ark of the Covenant of the Lord. Joshua 3: 3 says: "And they commanded the people, saying, when ye see the ark of the covenant of the LORD your God, and priests the Levites bearing it, then ye shall remove from your place, and go after it."

Back in the wilderness, when people rebelled against God, He sent plagues and consumed them with fire. After crossing the Jordan,

God trusted the people to make the right decisions, and they had to exercise their faith.

It was the priests who were to be the center of this act, while Joshua facilitated this miracle.

Crossing the Jordan represents moving from your flesh to your life in the spirit—transitioning from the law to the free gift of God's grace.

Two and a half tribes didn't want to cross the River Jordan. They settled for less because they couldn't grasp God's vision beyond the river. Their perspective was limited; they desired a mediocre life, much like many in the church today. You can't do anything for them; you can't force them or teach them. As someone said, "You can lead a horse to water, but you can't make him drink."

Only after you cross the Jordan are you qualified to fight your enemy.

Many have received a word from the Lord, yet years later, they are still waiting for its fulfillment. Many have completed their wilderness journey but have not crossed their Jordan yet. They still need visible evidence or feelings in order to do what God has asked them to do. They are unable to exercise their faith.

If you want to walk in God's destiny, you need to walk by faith, and not by sight.

CHAPTER 13

Overcoming a Spirit of Poverty

FAMINE OF LOVE

A major area that has been affected in the Body of Christ by this spirit of poverty are relationships. The evidence of this is a famine of true love in the Body of Christ.

The famine of love, in turn, is why there is a lack of material blessings.

God will withhold blessings and goodness from people, families, and churches that do not walk in unity and love.

The two greatest commandments in the Bible are to *Love the Lord your God with all your heart, soul, mind, and strength; and love your neighbor as yourself.*

When you claim to love God yet harbor grudges and offenses against your fellow brothers and sisters, you are a liar, and God is not within you:

> If someone says, "I love God," and hates his brother, he is a liar; for he who does not love his brother whom he has seen, how can he love God whom he has not seen? 1 John 4:20

> Behold, how good and how pleasant it is for brethren to dwell together in unity…For there the LORD commanded the blessing, even life forevermore. Psalm 133:1 & 13:3 (KJV)

Today, people are attempting to get rich at any cost. Thus, they offend others, and many break covenants and relationships. They cannot become wealthy because their actions are the opposite of true prosperity. They may work seven days a week, but still fall short of paying their bills and providing food for their children.

It is evident that a spirit of poverty needs to be uprooted from these lives and relationships.

Allow the love of God to flow through you to others who need it most—those who, in your opinion, don't deserve it. The individuals God sends into your life to bless you are often those who offend or ridicule you. Your response to them determines your destiny.

When you show love, kindness, and mercy to those who don't deserve it, you are interacting with the very people God has placed in your life to ignite His favor. They serve as catalysts for unleashing divine favor upon your life.

They are appointed by God to challenge you, as a way of teaching patience. Without patience you will achieve nothing for the kingdom of God. Instead, you will become a burden to the Body of Christ.

The Bible tells us that in the end, people will be arrogant and breakers of covenant (2 Timothy 3:1-5).

Today the body of Christ has a form of godliness, but no power. Perhaps this lack of power stems from a lack of love.

You don't need more prayer, fasting, or additional warfare conferences. You need to humble yourself and consider others better than yourself.

Interestingly, whenever the Bible says to be humble, it instructs you to take action personally. You can't ask God to make you humble. He won't do it. It's your choice, and you have to decide for yourself.

The devil works against humility. He is proud, haughty, arrogant, and stiff-necked.

SHOW GOD'S LOVE

You need to show the love of Christ to the world.

It is almost too late for the Body of Christ to wake up. People are caught up in and preoccupied with nonsense. While they are busy pulling down principalities and binding devils, they forget that the biggest devil resides between their two ears—in their minds.

The fortresses and strongholds of the enemy are not in the skies, but in the minds of people. You must have a breakthrough first in the earthly realm, before you can get victory in the heavens. Most people think the other way around.

Every action on earth has a reciprocal reaction in the heavens. If you obey God's Word on earth, God will send blessings from heaven. If you disobey the Word, He will send judgment from heaven.

When you walk in unity, humility, and love, the Lord opens the skies for you. However, some are trying to do it the other way around, to open the heavens in order to somehow bring love to us.

Love came down over 2,000 years ago and dwelt among us. He told us exactly what to do and how to walk in love. Jesus has shown you the same love His Father shows Him.

If Jesus loves you the same way the Father loves Him, common sense suggests that you would lack nothing in your own life. Would you experience a shortage of resources to fulfill His will? Certainly not.

You lack things today because you are poor, wretched, and naked—as He told the church in Laodicea. When you overcome the spirit of poverty in love and relationships, nothing can hold back the blessings of God.

Every obstacle you face in your Christian life is designed to reveal a little more of God to you. These challenges have been sent to help you know God.

Our God is a God Who hides (Isaiah 45:15). How does He hide? He hides behind problems, struggles, tests, offenses, and relationships. When you face these things in God's way, you will find Him.

It's like when you hide a toy from your children. It is already theirs, but you hide it to see if they are smart enough to find it. When they find that toy, they discover what was in your mind.

In the same way, God brings roadblocks into your path to see how you overcome them. When you overcome, you reveal God's secrets, His mind, and His love. These secrets represent principles of favor and love. The secret of the Lord is with those who love Him.

You must search for Him— as if searching for a hidden treasure, more precious than silver or gold. When you find Him, He is more precious than anything—gold, silver, diamonds, or rubies.

Many do not have time for Him today or for a relationship with Him. They are in a hurry to get rich. The more they make, the more they fall into temptation and get into debt.

1 Timothy 6:9 says: "But they that will be rich fall into temptation and a snare, and into many foolish and hurtful lusts, which drown men in destruction and perdition."

Even after retirement, they haven't fulfilled their financial dreams. They get disappointed and frustrated, and broken dreams are the end result. However, for humility and the fear of the Lord, you will get riches, honor, and life (Proverbs 22:4).

YOUR RELATIONSHIP WITH GOD AND OTHERS

Oh, dear child of God, listen to what He communicates through His word, from Genesis to Revelation. What matters to Him is your relationship with Him and with others.

Let's examine the relationship between Cain and Abel. They did not come together to worship. Cain held a grievance against his brother because Abel offered a better sacrifice than he did. Cain rebelled against God's order and was in rebellion against his brother as well. Abel brought a lamb to worship the Lord, but Cain refused to obey God's command. He further demonstrated his rebellion by opposing both God and his brother.

Let us consider what happened to Cain and his descendants. He was struck by the spirit of poverty and became a fugitive and wanderer on the earth:

> So now you are cursed from the earth, which has opened
> its mouth to receive your brother's blood from your

hand. When you till the ground, it shall no longer yield its strength to you. A fugitive and a vagabond you shall be on the earth. Genesis 4:11-12

Cain had a son called Enoch, which means "wandering." The rest of his descendants died in the flood, and his name was removed from the face of the earth.

Jesus said that when you bring an offering and know that your brother has something against you, keep the sacrifice and get reconciled to your brother, and then come back and offer your sacrifice.

In the Lord's Prayer, He said, as we forgive our debtors, so we are also forgiven (Matthew 6:12). "For with what judgment you judge, you will be judged; and with the measure you use, it will be measured back to you." (Matthew 7:2).

If you say you forgive and will not forget, God will do the same to you. God will respond accordingly if you say you forgive and never show any love and fellowship.

In the same way, God is not mocked. Whatsoever a man soweth, that shall he reap (Galatians 6: 7). In Revelation 2:23, Jesus says, "…I will give unto every one of you according to your works."

NO LONGER UNDER A SPIRIT OF POVERTY

Though He was holy and sinless, Jesus became sin to save you from sin. In the same way, He became poor, though rich, to deliver you from the curse of poverty:

> For you know the grace of our Lord Jesus Christ, that though He was rich, yet for your sakes He became poor, that you through His poverty might become rich. 2 Corinthians 8:9

Just like you don't have to be a sinner anymore unless, by choice, you don't have to be under the power of the spirit of poverty anymore.

Jesus Christ not only died for your sin and sickness, but also for your poverty; so that you need not lack the resources to fulfill His purpose.

Ephesians 3:19 says: "to know the love of Christ which passes knowledge; that you may be filled with all the fullness of God."

It is God's desire that you are filled with His fullness—lacking nothing. 1 Thessalonians 4:12: "That you may have lack of nothing."

God doesn't want you to be in lack, so why are you in that condition?

Instead, let's embrace what God has in store for you. Let's live the life of God.

LIVING HEAVEN'S LIFE ON EARTH

However, you cannot live Heaven's life on earth by following the laws of the earth. You need to follow the laws of Heaven.

This is what this book is going to help you to understand and do.

"The young lions lack and suffer hunger;
But those who seek the Lord shall not lack any
good thing." (Psalm 34:10)

God told the Israelites that the land He was leading them lacked nothing—everything was abundant.

This is not a book about becoming rich or wealthy, but about releasing God's resources in your life in order to fulfill His purpose and dream for you, as in Deuteronomy 8:7-9:

Easy and Light

God doesn't want you to carry any yoke on your back, except for the yoke of Christ, which is both easy and light. If you feel that the yoke of Christ is heavy and burdensome, then you need to seek help and deliverance from God and other anointed servants of the Lord.

God will never do anything in your life that goes against His Word. He is true to Himself and His Word. When He says His yoke will be easy and light, that is exactly what He means.

Jesus will never make you carry a cross that is too heavy for you. He has made each of us, and He knows what you are capable of enduring. He will never let you be tempted beyond what you can bear (1 Corinthians 10:13).

The Pharisees placed burdens on people that they could not carry, and they never helped bear them. Jesus came to set the captives free to help you fulfill the purpose and plan that God has ordained for your life.

Anyone bound by the spirit of poverty will never be able to completely fulfill God's purpose. They will live in continuous disappointment and die disappointed. However, God created you to live joyfully and die satisfied fulfilled.

For God's children, freedom is now—not some day in the future. the Israelites waited some 430 years!

For you, Jesus finished the work on the cross so that you can obtain freedom any time you want it. You don't have to wait for Him or anyone else, as freedom has been legally made available to you. You need only to appropriate it.

I want to highlight some scripture references that show the spirit of poverty has no more power over those who are redeemed by the blood of the Lamb:

- Philippians 2:30
- Deuteronomy 2: 7
- 1 Kings 4:27, 9:21
- 1 Samuel 30:19
- Jeremiah 23:4

- Luke 22:35
- 2 Corinthians 11:9
- 1 Corinthians 16:17
- Hebrews 4:1
- 2 Corinthians 8:2

CHAPTER 14

The Patriarchs

We are going to learn from the lives of the patriarchs[2] of our faith and how they overcame this spirit of poverty

They are called *fathers* because they came before us in faith and knowledge. Children learn from their fathers. In Galatians chapter three, we are called the children of Abraham. Our God is the God of Abraham, Isaac, and Jacob.

While they were not perfect, as we are not perfect, we can still learn from their examples, as well as from their mistakes—so that we won't have to repeat them.

CARE FOR RELATIONSHIPS

When we study the lives of mighty men and women of God in the Bible, we notice some common characteristics—they were all very

---

2 Fathers (of our Faith)

careful about their relationships. How they managed their relationships was more important to them than how they managed their own lives.

It seems that they all understood the pain a broken relationship could cause. They recognized that if there was a broken relationship in their lives, God's favor would not flow freely. They acted wisely regarding personal offenses.

David had a similar experience with King Saul. The way he dealt with Saul was crucial to David's breakthrough. The defeat of Goliath brought material blessings to David, but the way he treated Saul brought anointing to his life. Anointing flows when you walk in God's love. The Bible instructs us to love our enemies.

BREAKING EVERY CURSE

We are going to see how love breaks every curse and evil spirit. God is a God of love. He is love. He loved the world and sent His only begotten Son to save us. The Bible says that love covers a multitude of sins (1 Peter 4:8). Perfect love casts out all fear (1 John 4:18).

If sin and fear can be gone because of love, then with love in your life there will be no place for the devil to work. He can only come into your life through sin which is his entrance.

The most important commandment in the Bible is to love God, and then to love others as you love yourself. Jesus stated that this encompasses the teachings of both the prophets and the law.

In Genesis 12:2-3, God told Abraham: "I will make you a great nation; I will bless you, and make your name great; and you shall be a blessing. I will bless those who bless you, and I will curse him who curses you; and in you all the families of the earth shall be blessed."

The word 'bless' in Hebrew does not mean what we usually say and think. When we sing, "I will bless thee Oh, Lord," what does that mean? How do we bless the Lord?

Psalm 34:1 says, **"I will bless the Lord at all times."** In both these cases the same Hebrew word is used. When God said to Abraham that He would bless him and make his name great, what was really in His mind?

The Hebrew word for *bless* is "Barak," meaning to kneel, congratulate, praise, salute or thank.[3]

Does that mean God will kneel, congratulate, praise, salute, or thank Abraham?

This was a promise of the Messiah, the Son of man, Who would be born as the Seed of Abraham. The Bible says that even though Abraham received the promise, he died without entering the rest (Hebrews 11:39-40). At the same time, Abraham enjoyed the benefit of it.

THE LIMITLESS WORD OF GOD

When God speaks, His Word is not limited by time. His Word is not limited by tense. His Word doesn't have past, present, or future. Rather, His Word endures forever, even to a thousand generations.

When God gives you a Word, that Word will not die with you. When you die, it is passed on to your children and to a thousand

---

3 Strong's 1288

generations. You live in it and pass it on to your children. When it goes from your generation to the next, the blessings increase. The Word multiplies.

Whatever God does is always in progression and growth. His Word is constantly in motion. It's like receiving a seed; when you plant it, you will get more seeds, and the seed's traits are limitless. One word from the mouth of God holds limitless potential.

Make Thy Name Great

This truly came to fruition in the life of Jesus. God gave Him a name that is above every other name:

> Therefore God also has highly exalted Him and given Him the name which is above every name,

> That at the name of Jesus every knee should bow, of those in heaven, and of those on earth, and of those under the earth," Philippians 2:9 &10

You may kneel now, or you will kneel later. Jesus, who will rule the nations with a rod of iron, will make everyone kneel before Him. All who will not kneel before Jesus shall be cut off.

Isaiah 41:12 says You shall seek them and not find them. Those who contended with you. Those who war against you shall be as nothing, As a nonexistent thing.

"I will bless them that bless you."

God is saying I will honor and respect them that respect you. If you honor God, He will honor you (1 Samuel 2:30). He will curse those who curse thee.

"and in you all the families of the earth shall be blessed."

This is the promise of Abraham (Genesis 12:3).

Egypt Mindset

When Abraham came out obeying God's call, the first obstacle he faced was a famine in the land (Genesis 12:10). The spirit of poverty came against him. When Abraham faced this principality, he made the wrong decision and took the wrong route by going to Egypt, the land of poverty.

One goal of the spirit of poverty is to keep you in Egypt and turn you back to your old ways.

When Isaac faced the same problem, God appeared to him and instructed him not to go to Egypt (Genesis 26:2). The people of Israel exhibited the same attitude when they left Egypt. Although they had been delivered from Egypt, they were not free from the spirit of Egypt. We refer to this as the mindset of Egypt.

Just because you are saved does not mean that all demons have departed from you or that you are free from evil spirits. Do not be deceived. After you are saved, the next step is deliverance from evil spirits. Otherwise, they will taunt and oppress you, keeping you away from your Promised Land.

The spirit of poverty brings lack, scarcity, and famine into your life, and cause you to complain against God, which He does not appreciate. His anger can turn against you and result in your destruction from the face of the earth.

This spirit of poverty opens doors to many other demons that serve under it, such as complaining, murmuring, backbiting, hatred, idolatry, witchcraft, adultery, fornication, murder, lust, destruction, lack, impoverishment, exhaustion, debt, tiredness, hopelessness, famine, disunity, laziness, slothfulness, and fatigue.

Even if you are financially well-off, you need to be careful by guarding yourself against this spirit. Its purpose is to rob you of

God's blessings. It will try to lead you into trouble in some other area of life—to make an entry for a demon. If one demon gets into your life, others can easily follow.

One area where the devil works on those who have money is in their relationships. Abraham was rich in gold, silver, and livestock. The problem arose in Genesis 13:5-7, when there wasn't enough space for both his herds and Lot's cattle to dwell and graze together. Strife broke out between their servants.

Do you realize that when there is strife between your servants and someone else's servants, it affects both masters as well?

> So Abram said to Lot, "Please let there be no strife between you and me, and between my herdsmen and your herdsmen; for we are brethren. Genesis 13:8

While Abraham tried to protect Lot, it seemed he was more focused on their material wealth. This caused a rift in their relationship, leading them to part ways.

Abraham had God's promise to protect him, which meant Lot was safe as long as he stayed with Abraham. Once he left, however, Lot became vulnerable to the enemy's attacks. Consequently, Lot chose to settle in Sodom and Gomorrah.

Whenever you act against the Word of God, you open a door for the enemy. Lot moved away from his spiritual covering and didn't seek reconciliation with Abraham or his servants. He seemed indifferent to Abraham and his servants.

Lot's goal was to accumulate wealth—similar to many today. He prioritized worldly riches over Abraham's calling or mission. His focus was trapped in the pursuit of worldly wealth (1 Timothy 6:9).

In Genesis chapter 14, we see that pagan kings invaded Sodom and Gomorrah, plundering all the goods and capturing Lot, his family, and his possessions.

When Abraham learned of this, he could have easily thought, "Yes, I warned Lot that if he left me, he would be on his own. Don't bother me anymore." However, he didn't share the same mindset as many Christians do today.

Abraham didn't say the usual, "I told you so," or, "I will pray that God sends His angels to deliver you." No, Abraham had a heart like God's; he was called the friend of God. Abraham didn't think that just because Lot was gone, he could stop loving him.

Breakthrough in Abraham's Life

Even though Lot went his own way, Abraham's love for him didn't diminish. Even though you turn away from God, He doesn't stop loving you. You may have offended Him in many ways, but He always came to your rescue, even at times when you were living in sin.

God took the initiative to redeem you, even though you were the one who strayed from Him. This is why Christ commanded you to go to the brother who offended you and be reconciled to him—not to wait until he or she comes to you.

Abraham went with the mighty men from his own house. He was willing to sacrifice his own resources to redeem his brother who had walked away from him. He could have easily hired other people. He had the money to do it. Instead, he put his very life at risk, and took his best men, and went to save his brother who had forsaken him.

You may have thought or asked what you would get out of it if you did that for him; he wasn't even thankful for what I had already done for him; what if the lives of my servants are lost, and that loss affects my business?

Abraham had a different spirit. He went and fought with those kings and rescued Lot and all he had. Jesus said, "Greater love has no one than this, than to lay down one's life for his friends." (John 15:13).

This is the true test of every child of God—when you go out to bless or rescue someone who has not been nice to you, or respectful to you; or, perhaps they spoke evil of you.

When you do what is pleasing to God, all of heaven moves on your behalf. God is a righteous Judge. He loves righteousness and justice. His justice, however, is a little different from our justice.

He loves all of His creation. He is merciful and long-suffering (Psalm 145:8, Psalm 86:15, Exodus 34:6). When you express His nature in and through your life, His favor and abundance become your reward. He will not withhold any good thing from your life.

Now, when Abraham came back victorious from the battle, something powerful happened to his life. Someone came to meet him and salute him.

Many people discuss this event in the context of tithing and manipulate people about giving. They don't fully understand why Melchizedek came to meet Abraham.

Abraham gave all he had and put at risk his best servants and almost everything he owned. Heaven said, we can sit here and just watch this. God sent one of His special Ambassadors from heaven to meet and greet him.

When you move out to help your brother or sister who is in need and who may not be your favorite, even kings will bow to you (Genesis 14:17).

Melchizedek, the priest of the Most High God, brought bread and wine and Abraham had communion with Melchizedek (Genesis 14:18-20).

I believe it was Jesus Christ, Himself, Who appeared to him.

He blessed Abraham again and, in blessing, kneeled and acknowledged His wisdom and love; because Abraham once again discovered a divine secret of prosperity, health, and obedience.

Abraham broke that curse of hatred and strife in his life with Lot by going the extra mile. He broke that poverty of lack of love. I believe it was a big lesson for Lot to learn.

After this God appeared to Abraham and said that He will be his shield and his exceedingly great reward (Genesis 15:1). God Himself became his shield, not his money or servants.

A shield is that which protects you from the enemy's assaults and attacks, arrows, and swords. Abraham could now be safe and secure because God was taking care of all his affairs.

GOD'S LOVE IN ACTION

God will fight for you when you show love and compassion to the needy (Proverbs 19:17). When God protects you, everything you have is safe and secure.

Jesus told us the parable of the Good Samaritan, which deals with the question, "Who is your neighbor?"

Whoever is in need is your neighbor, regardless of color, creed, religion, or nationality. Everyone is a part of God's creation; if they are in need, you are supposed to help them.

Our God is a God of relationships. His priority is relationships. Everything in the Kingdom of God flows through relationships.

We are all members of the same body. Jesus said in Luke 17:2, "it would be better for him if a millstone were hung around his neck, and he were thrown into the sea, than that he should offend one of these little ones."

Nothing is more important to God than your relationships with Him and others. Your victory or your defeat is based on your relationships.

The enemy has worked a great breach in the kingdom and church, dividing it into as many pieces as possible, as well as many little kingdoms and kings and some queens.

Everything from God flows through relationships. We are supposed to be like the Godhead in both relationship and unity (John 17:23).

Because Abraham dared and took that step to save his brother (Genesis 14:14-16), his life afterward was never the same. His relationship with God was never the same. It was only after this incident that God established His covenant with Abraham. Until then, it was just a promise.

In chapter fifteen of Genesis, God established His covenant with Abraham, and told him about his future. When you take that first step to mend that broken relationship, it is the first step to true prosperity.

When all of your relationships with others are based on God's Word, you are safe from all the attacks of the enemy. The enemy will not have any ground to launch an attack against you or accuse you before God. When there is no enemy, you live in peace.

The Bible says, "If it is possible, live in peace with all" (Romans 12:18).

Now, as soon as Abraham achieved victory over that attack, the devil began causing trouble in his home. The devil suggested a 'good idea' to Sarai (whose name was changed to Sarah in Genesis 17:15), to give her maid to Abraham to bear him an heir (Genesis 16:1-6).

Abraham, *the man of faith,* fell into his wife's plan and slept with Hagar. Once the devil saw that his plan had worked, he returned to harass Sarah with a sense of guilt and condemnation.

Once again, strife and contention began in their family life (verses 5 & 6). So, Sarah chased Hagar out of the house when she was pregnant with Abraham's son.

While Hagar was in the wilderness, God appeared to her and told her to go back and submit herself to Sarah and do whatever she says. That meant that if Sarah were to mistreat her, Hagar could not resist. Why?

God in His sovereignty knows that if there is strife and contention in Abraham's life, the promise cannot be fulfilled. God was poised to move on Abraham's behalf after a long period of waiting.

The devil understands God's timing, and therefore he attempts to create a breach in relationships. Two dangerous spirits operate under the spirit of poverty: abortion and barrenness. Their aim is to delay God's timing and undermine His promises for your life.

The spirit of abortion can derail your harvest, divine appointments, relationships, and much more. Its plan is to disrupt and delay the process before you give birth to God's vision. This spirit seeks to thwart your breakthroughs in the spiritual realm. If they are intercepted in the spirit realm, you will never be able to realize them. They resemble intercepting missiles that target God's blessings in transit.

God has blessed you with all spiritual blessings in Christ in heavenly places (Ephesians 1:3). God has already blessed you with every blessing you need or will ever need. Now, they have to come to you by breaking through the enemy's barriers.

The devil is known as the prince of the power of the air. He and his minions work in the air.

Before the blessing gets to you, it can be intercepted, delayed, scattered, dried up, and exhausted.

ALL AUTHORITY OVER THE ENEMY

You need to thwart the enemy's plans by destroying them. (Jeremiah 1:10). You have authority over all the power of the enemy (Luke 10:19). 2 Corinthians 2:11 states that we are not ignorant of his devices.

God also pronounced a blessing on Hagar's child. Abraham was eighty-six years old when Ishmael was born to him. I believe that God's purpose and promise to Abraham were delayed because of a broken relationship. We may refer to it as unbelief or disobedience.

We don't hear of any communication between God and Abraham for the next thirteen years following Ishmael's birth.

When he was ninety-nine years old, God appeared to him again. Perhaps it took this long to heal the wounds in their hearts. One thing that can prevent you from hearing God or Him speaking to you is the hurt and offense in your heart.

Matthew 5:8 reminds us that the pure in heart shall see God. However, God is faithful to His Word—even when you are unfaithful. What He has promised, He will do if you allow Him to mold you and shape you.

You can rebel against God's plan and miss it. That doesn't mean you can do whatever you want, because God will ultimately fulfill what He has spoken. No, that goes totally against God's Word and His principles.

Abraham had decided to settle for second best (Genesis 17:18), and became mediocre. Even though the Bible doesn't credit the devil, you can see his influence behind this situation. Therefore, we should never give any credit to his destructive works, but rather dismantle them as Jesus of Nazareth did (1 John 3:8).

God established a physical sign of circumcision for Abraham to remind him of His covenant. Every time he saw the circumcision, he thought about God's promises.

To prevent any further breaches in their relationship, Hagar and Ishmael stayed with Abraham until Isaac was born.

Sometimes, you need to endure the messes of others, not just for their benefit, but to ensure your blessings aren't delayed. Patience is the key to entering God's Promised Land (Hebrews 6:12).

In chapter 18 of Genesis, God appeared to Abraham once again. Another test was presented to him in the areas of love and giving. Three men stood by the way, whom Abraham invited in, showing love and hospitality by giving them the best of what he had. God blessed him again and reassured him of His promise.

The following year, Abraham and Sarah experienced the fulfill-ment of their long-awaited dream.

It is astonishing to see that giving precedes most miracles in the Bible.

BREAKTHROUGH IN ISAAC'S LIFE

Blessings are generational, as are curses. There are generational curses as well as generational blessings. One act of obedience or disobedience will have eternal consequences.

You may tend to commit the same mistakes or sins that your father committed. There is a default setting in your nature that you inherited from your parents: a propensity to fail where they failed. Unless you take care of that purposefully and specifically, things won't work out well.

You see this in the patriarch's lives—that these principles manifested in their lives from one generation to the next.

Abraham went to Egypt during a famine in the land, and when Isaac encountered the same problem, he also intended to go to Egypt. However, God intervened and stopped him. Abraham lied about his wife, and Isaac did the same. When it came to Jacob, he too told many lies.

In Genesis 21:27, we see that Abraham made a covenant with Abimelech, the king of Gerar (a Philistine city-state). When it was time for Isaac, his relationship with Abimelech did not go well.

During another famine in the land, Isaac sowed and reaped a hundredfold. God blessed him in everything he did (Genesis 26:12-13). The Philistines envied him because of his blessings. Today, we often envy the ungodly when we see their prosperity. In Isaac's time, the ungodly envied him. Witnessing Isaac's growth and prosperity instilled fear in Abimelech, leading him to ask Isaac to leave the land:

> And Abimelech said to Isaac, "Go away from us, for you
> are much mightier than we." (Genesis 26:16)

You need to remember that Abraham made a covenant with Abimelech. A covenant is eternal. You cannot break a covenant. When you break a covenant, favor lifts, and poverty walks in.

Until now, Isaac had no problems in his life. Isaac was prosperous—even in a time of famine. After he left Abimelech and tried to dig the wells that his father had dug, strife broke out between his servants and the men of Gerar (Genesis 26:20).

Strife is not a sign of blessing and favor, as strife gives an open door for the enemy.

Isaac had an encounter with God in Genesis 26:24-25:

> And the Lord appeared to him the same night and said, "I am the God of your father Abraham; do not fear, for I am with you. I will bless you and multiply your descendants for My servant Abraham's sake."
>
> So he built an altar there and called on the name of the Lord, and he pitched his tent there; and there Isaac's servants dug a well.

Following this, Abimelech came back to meet Isaac as written in Genesis 26:26-27:

> Then Abimelech came to him from Gerar with Ahuzzath, one of his friends, and Phichol the commander of his army. And Isaac said to them, "Why have you come to me, since you hate me and have sent me away from you?"

Abimelech and his men came to reconcile and renew the covenant. They said:

> But they said, "We have certainly seen that the Lord is with you. So we said, 'Let there now be an oath between us, between you and us; and let us make a covenant with you,'" (Genesis 26:28).

They made a covenant and restored the broken relationship. Favor was restored to Isaac and his life. The same day, Isaac's servants told him they found water:

It came to pass the same day that Isaac's servants came and told him about the well which they had dug, and said to him, "We have found water." (Genesis 26:32).

Breakthrough in Jacob's Life

By name, he was a supplanter and a deceiver, yet God had something different in His heart for Jacob. Before God blessed him, he had to pass the test of love to inherit the promise.

There are three tests you and I need to pass if we are going to inherit God's promise.

The Test of Money

You will be tested in the area of money before you are financially blessed. Love for the world—the Bible calls it the pride of life, and self-indulgence—are parts of the love of money.

Jesus said, if He could not trust you with earthly treasure, He couldn't trust you with heaven's treasure (Luke 16:11).

Money should not be the goal in your life. The love of money is the root of all evil. Rather, money is a means to get things done. Money is a reward when you walk in God's call. Money is a reward when you solve someone else's problem.

The Test of the Flesh

You will be tested in the area of sex. Both men and women will be tested in this area.

Sexual sins have more consequences than some other sins, because they both defile your spirit, soul, and body; and destroy your confidence. The repercussions of sexual sins can extend up to ten generations.

Everyone will be tempted and tested repeatedly in this area. As long as you are alive, the flesh will raise its ugly head and will try to get you into temptation.

The Test of Love

This is the hardest one to overcome. It is easy to love someone who is nice to you and has the same social status.

I have heard people say they love India, yet they have never been there. Only when they visit India will their love be tested, and then they will know for sure whether their love was true or not. I have included this test in the last chapter.

Jesus said to love your enemies, and bless those who curse you, and pray for those who spitefully use and persecute you (Matthew 5:44).

Jacob was a deceiver. He deceived his brother and took his birthright. He deceived his father and inherited the blessing. As a result, Esau was so full of wrath toward him that he sought to kill him. Esau said he would wait until the death of his father, and then kill Jacob.

Following his mother's advice, Jacob ran away from home and dwelt in Haran. There he worked for his mother's brother, feeding his flock. Laban, Rebecca's father, was a subtle man who made Jacob work for him for fourteen years before he allowed him to marry his two daughters. (Genesis 29).

Jacob began to reap what he sowed in his life, and thus was deceived by Laban. He spent a total of twenty years with Laban in Haran—fourteen years for his wives and a further six years for the cattle (Genesis 31: 38, 41).

How many of us realize that you cannot run away from problems? You have to confront them sooner or later. The problem you avoid will eventually catch up with you.

Offense and hurt will not heal by simply changing locations, as these are matters of the heart. Even if you change your house or the place you live, you can't change what's in your heart. The sooner you face it, the better your life will be.

Before Jacob fled, he spoke to his father and clarified things. Isaac blessed him once more and sent him away to Haran (Genesis 28:1). However, the issue with his brother remained unresolved.

After twenty years, when he departed from Haran, he didn't leave in peace with Laban. God, in His mercy, didn't let another offense come into his life. Laban came back to meet Jacob. They reconciled and made a covenant together (Genesis 31:44).

Though he worked hard and earned some material blessings, he had not yet inherited the promise that God had made with his fathers. The spiritual breakthrough in Jacob's life had not yet come.

The reason was that the relationship with his brother was not yet restored. The offense was still active between them.

One day, Jacob decided to return to his country and reconcile with his brother. As he was journeying to meet his brother, he had to cross a river called Jabbok. In the evening, he let all his family, servants, and flocks cross the river ahead of him while he was left alone on the side of the brook.

That same night, he decided to reconcile and mend his relationship with his brother. A Man came to wrestle with him till the break of the day:

> And Jacob was left alone; and there wrestled a Man with him until the breaking of the day. Genesis 32:24

The wrestling continued into the early morning, but Jacob refused to let go of the Man until he received the blessing. In truth, he was wrestling with God for his breakthrough. God was engaging with him to transform his nature.

When God knew that Jacob was not going to let go, He blessed him and changed his name from Jacob to Israel, meaning the prince of God:

> And He said, "Your name shall no longer be called Jacob, but Israel; for you have struggled with God and with men, and have prevailed." Genesis 32:28

The long-awaited breakthrough in Jacob's life came the very night he decided to reconcile with his brother Esau. Now, he was going to meet Esau, not as the old Jacob, but as Israel.

When you release forgiveness and love to those who deserve it the least, you are demonstrating God's nature and likeness through your life. God will come down to honor you and lift you up to a new position and your long-awaited miracle will occur in your life.

Do you see now why the enemy's strategy involves breaking up relationships and bringing offenses between people? He comes to steal God's favor and blessing from you. He mostly does this through broken relationships, broken covenants, broken commitments, and broken promises. May the Lord open your eyes and help you to walk in love.

YOUR *LOT*, OR *SAUL*, OR *ESAU*, OR *JUDAS* AND *PETER*

God will send you some "Lots" in your life. They come not to hurt you, but to bless you. There will be some "Esaus" as well. They are there to change and promote you. Without them, you can't receive the blessing. Without them, you can't have God's favor.

The people you thought came to hurt you are actually there to bring blessings. They are the keys that open doors no one else can unlock for you. Everyone sees the rock, but few see the sculpture within. All will pass by, but the person who takes the time to chisel away the excess will create a beautiful piece of artwork.

God will send you a *Judas* as well as a *Peter*. Both are necessary for your growth and promotion. Without Judas, Jesus would have been unable to fulfill the scriptures. Without Peter, the door to the Gentiles would not have been opened.

It is your responsibility to recognize the essential roles of a "Peter" and "Judas" in your life. Most people welcome *Peter* and try to avoid *Judas*, so they end up with one-sided blessings. If only one of your legs kept growing, what would happen? Both need to grow to be the same size.

Many people know how to handle money but are poor managers of people. Others may be good with people, but bad with money. You need the Word and prayer. Both need to be in balance in your life.

God allowed the devil's continued existence because His divine plan includes using even opposition to fulfill His greater purpose, while keeping us humble in spirit. A messenger of Satan was given to Paul. If it weren't for the devil, some might not even be Christians today. What the enemy meant for evil, God will turn around as a blessing.

Saul was sent to David to promote him—not to destroy him. David would have been ruined if he had approached Saul with the wrong attitude. It is easy to defeat Goliath, someone you can kill, but Saul is different; you must love and honor him.

There are two types of enemies that enter your life. One who seeks to destroy you, requiring you to eliminate him first; however, the other is there to promote you. While you will receive blessings from dealing with both, many men and women of God have missed out on numerous blessings because they mistreated their *Lot*, or *Judas*, or *Saul*, or *Esau*.

You need not worry about these types of people. God will handle them, because He is the One directing them your way. If you treat them kindly, they will not bring about your destruction; instead, they will lead to their own downfall.

Your response to them shapes your destiny. You will be blessed without having to engage with these individuals, but your blessing will be limited. Your influence in the kingdom will also be constrained.

There is a difference between the Philistines and Judas. Sometimes, you need to keep a 'Judas' close, even if you dislike him or recognize his intentions to hinder you. He is essential. Without him, you cannot achieve your highest potential.

EXTRAORDINARY PEOPLE

Extraordinary people treat others extraordinarily. Extraordinary people achieve extraordinary things.

There are not very many people who want to go all the way with God. As soon as they face a lion or bear on their way they will retreat to their own caves. They will try to keep others in the cave also.

David's brothers tried to stop him from facing Goliath. They tried, and failed; and they didn't want anyone else to try, because they had already drawn the conclusion that Goliath was undefeatable. They hadn't killed their own lions and bears before.

These are the people who are afraid, and run from their lions and bears. However, David had already dealt with similar challenges before, so he knew how to take care of Goliath. It was the same way, with God's help.

If you can't defeat your own enemies, don't try to help others overcome theirs. If you do, you will end up in great trouble. This is why David became their greatest enemy.

The limit of the open skies above you depend on the enemies you overcome in your life. The amount of love you receive from God correlates with the love you are willing to give to others.

Many want big blessings from God, but they give small blessings. You can't pour four gallons of milk into a one-gallon bottle. No matter how you try, three gallons will be lost. Many people's hearts and minds are as small as a one-gallon bottle, yet they ask God to pour into them more than they can contain.

Enlarge your heart toward others, and God will enlarge your blessings. If you sow sparingly, you will reap sparingly. If you sow generously, you will reap generously. If you sow large blessings to others, God will pour out extra-large blessings on you.

Whatsoever a man sows, that shall he reap

If you are ready to show extraordinary love to others, God will show extraordinary love to you. God is not mocked. Why did God bless Solomon with riches and wisdom? It was because he had a heart so large, as vast as the sand on the seashore. (1 Kings 4:29).

When you give $100 to the Lord, if it feels like a sacrifice, then what would happen if He told you to give $1000? You might feel overwhelmed! God will only enlarge your heart if you ask and cooperate with Him.

Your sacrifice becomes acceptable to God whenever you sacrifice something for someone else. Jesus said, "And whosoever shall compel thee to go a mile, go with him twain" (Matthew 5:41 KJV). If someone slaps you on the cheek, show the other cheek as well. Lord, help us to follow in Your footsteps.

In Matthew 18:7 Jesus said:

> Woe to the world because of offenses! For offenses must come, but woe to that man by whom the offense comes!

Offense is not good, but it must happen for the good of those who face it; yet it brings destruction to those by whom it comes. It is terrible for those who bring offense into our lives, though it is a means that blesses us when we deal with it with God's heart; but woe to those by whom the offense comes.

CHAPTER 15

Help the Poor and Needy

It doesn't matter how much you fast and pray or cast out demons; there are some breakthroughs that do not come until you step out to help the poor.

God has always had a special place in His heart for the cries of the poor, orphans, and widows. He is known as the *God of the fatherless and widows.*

Some of the wealthiest people on this earth became wealthy because they, or their business, always have an outreach to the hurting and the poor.

Jesus knows what it is to be born into a poor family. He became poor so that we can be wealthy (2 Corinthians 8:9). Even though poverty is a curse, you are positioned to help the poor so that you can get blessed.

It doesn't matter how many welfare and social programs the government or UN may run, God says the poor shall never cease from out of the land. He said this to His people whom He brought out of slavery and into a land that flows with milk and honey. Even in a land where He commanded His best, He said the poor would still be present. Why?

Deuteronomy 15:7-11 says:

> If there is among you a poor man of your brethren, within any of the gates in your land which the Lord your God is giving you, you shall not harden your heart nor shut your hand from your poor brother, but you shall open your hand wide to him and willingly lend him sufficient for his need, whatever he needs.
>
> Beware lest there be a wicked thought in your heart, saying, "The seventh year, the year of release, is at hand," and your eye be evil against your poor brother and you give him nothing, and he cry out to the Lord against you, and it become sin among you.
>
> You shall surely give to him, and your heart should not be grieved when you give to him, because for this thing the Lord your God will bless you in all your works and in all to which you put your hand.
>
> For the poor will never cease from the land; therefore I command you, saying, "You shall open your hand wide to your brother, to your poor and your needy, in your land."

In the verse above, God is saying that when you help the poor with an open heart, God shall bless the works of your hands. That is a means of breaking poverty off your hands. If the work of your hands needs to prosper, you need to use your hands to help the poor and needy.

The widow in Elijah's day was poor and ready to die because of poverty in her house, but one act of giving broke that curse off her life, and she was blessed for the rest of her life.

Again, God says in Deuteronomy 26:12 that: "Then Isaac sowed in that land, and reaped in the same year a hundredfold; and the Lord blessed him."

I had never heard this teaching before. All I knew was to bring the tithes to the storehouse. I had never heard a preacher say we must give our tithes not only to the Levites but also to the stranger, the fatherless, and the widow. No wonder many who faithfully tithe do not experience their breakthrough, even after tithing for many years!

You may say, Abraham, doesn't God say in the book of Malachi to bring the tithes into the storehouse? Yes, He did, but for what reason? Let us read that scripture with our eyes open. Malachi 3:10 says: Bring all the tithes into the storehouse, that there may be food in My house, and "try Me now in this," says the Lord of hosts, "If I will not open for you the windows of heaven and pour out for you such blessing that there will not be room enough to receive it."

The number one reason God said to bring the tithes to the storehouse was to have meat in the storehouse. Why does God's storehouse need meat?

It is for the stranger, the fatherless, the widow, and the needy. When they come hungry, looking for something to eat; and if God's storehouse is empty, where else can they go?

You may say, isn't this speaking about spiritual food? Certainly not, because when a hungry and naked person comes to you, you don't speak in *tongues and prophesy to him; you meet his physical needs first.*

You read the same thing in the book of James. James 2:15-16 says:

If a brother or sister is naked and destitute of daily food, and one of you says to them, "Depart in peace, be warmed and filled," but you do not give them the things which are needed for the body, what does it profit?

If a part of your tithes doesn't go to feed the hungry and clothe the naked, you will not be blessed to the measure God says in His Word. If your tithes go only to pay the mortgage of the building, TV and radio stations, and printing materials for fundraising, let me tell you, you are being used and deceived by men.

May the Lord open your eyes to see the truth, because the Lord says: 'you shall know the truth and the truth shall set you free.'

BENEFITS OF HELPING THE POOR

There are significant benefits which come into play when you help the poor. These include the following:

Financial Breakthrough

Proverbs 19:17 says: "He who has pity on the poor lends to the Lord, and He will pay back what he has given."

The scripture above says when you give to the poor, you are lending to the LORD. When you lend to the Lord, He will pay you back at the highest interest rate in your time of need.

Who are the Poor?

You really need to understand who the poor are. Not everyone in need is necessarily poor.

Some are poor because they are too lazy and do not want to move their bodies. The poor, in God's eyes, are those who cannot help themselves, the unfortunate, without an opportunity, even if they want to improve their situation.

One simple test to distinguish between the poor and the lazy is this: The poor will accept your advice, but the lazy will make an excuse or rebel against your words. The poor want to improve, but the lazy want to stay the same forever.

Debt-Free Living

Proverbs 28:27 says: "He who gives to the poor will not lack, But he who hides his eyes will have many curses."

If you ignore the cry of the poor, you may cry yourself and not receive any answer. There could be many other reasons why your prayer may not be answered. One of them could be that you are not answering the cry of the poor.

One of the timeless principles of the Word of God, is helping the poor. Both the Old Testament and New Testament are equally important for understanding how to help the poor.

Jesus said in Luke 4:18, "The Spirit of the Lord is upon Me, because He has anointed Me to preach the gospel to the poor;…"

Why do the poor need the gospel?

The gospel is good news that assures the poor they can be freed from their poverty and break the curse off their lives.

Healing from Sickness

Psalm 41:1-3 says: "Blessed is he who considers the poor; the Lord will deliver him in time of trouble. The Lord will preserve him and keep him alive, and he will be blessed on the earth; You will not deliver him to the will of his enemies the Lord will strengthen him on his bed of illness; You will sustain him on his sickbed."

Six Further Blessings

For those who assist the poor, there are at least six blessings concealed in the scripture above. Here they are, listed one by one:

1) **Your deliverance in the time of trouble**

2) **The Lord will preserve and keep you alive**

3) **You shall be blessed upon the earth**

4) **God will defeat your enemies**

5) **Strength in times of weakness**

6) **Your healing.**

Prosperity

Deuteronomy 15: 7-11 says: "If there is among you a poor man of your brethren, within any of the gates in your land which the Lord your God is giving you, you shall not harden your heart nor shut your hand from your poor brother, but you shall open your hand wide to him and willingly lend him sufficient for his need, whatever he needs. Beware lest there be a wicked thought in your heart, saying, 'The seventh year, the year of release, is at hand,' and your eye be evil against your poor brother and you give him nothing, and he cry out to the Lord against you, and it become sin among you. You shall surely give to him, and your heart should not be grieved when you give to him, because for this thing the Lord your God will bless you in all your works and in all to which you put your hand. For the poor will never cease from the land; therefore I command you, saying, 'You shall open your hand wide to your brother, to your poor and your needy, in your land.'"

The scripture above says God will bless you in all your works and everything you put your hands to do.

Prosperity is not just financial abundance. True prosperity is a life filled with peace and joy regardless of the circumstances. Many are financially blessed, but they are miserable, and do not have peace of mind.

When you are prosperous you will be like a tree that was planted by the riverside (Psalm 1:3).

Inheritance in the Kingdom of God

Jesus has said much in this regard, so I am not going to explain this any further, other than to quote just what He said in Matthew 25:31-45:

> When the Son of Man comes in His glory, and all the holy angels with Him, then He will sit on the throne of His glory.
>
> All the nations will be gathered before Him, and He will separate them one from another, as a shepherd divides his sheep from the goats. And He will set the sheep on His right hand, but the goats on the left.
>
> Then the King will say to those on His right hand, "Come, you blessed of My Father, inherit the kingdom prepared for you from the foundation of the world: for I was hungry and you gave Me food; I was thirsty and you gave Me drink; I was a stranger and you took Me in; I was naked and you clothed Me; I was sick and you visited Me; I was in prison and you came to Me."
>
> Then the righteous will answer Him, saying, "Lord, when did we see You hungry and feed You, or thirsty and give You drink? When did we see You a stranger and take You in, or naked and clothe You? Or when did we see You sick, or in prison, and come to You?"

And the King will answer and say to them, "Assuredly, I say to you, inasmuch as you did it to one of the least of these My brethren, you did it to Me."

Then He will also say to those on the left hand, "Depart from Me, you cursed, into the everlasting fire prepared for the devil and his angels: for I was hungry and you gave Me no food; I was thirsty and you gave Me no drink; I was a stranger and you did not take Me in, naked and you did not clothe Me, sick and in prison and you did not visit Me."

Then they also will answer Him, saying, "Lord, when did we see You hungry or thirsty or a stranger or naked or sick or in prison, and did not minister to You?"

Then He will answer them, saying, "Assuredly, I say to you, inasmuch as you did not do it to one of the least of these, you did not do it to Me." And these will go away into everlasting punishment, but the righteous into eternal life.

We are called not only to see and enter the kingdom of God, but to inherit it.

Inherit Eternal Life

Mark 10:17-22 says:

Now as He was going out on the road, one came running, knelt before Him, and asked Him, "Good Teacher, what shall I do that I may inherit eternal life?"

So Jesus said to him, "Why do you call Me good? No one is good but One, that is, God.

You know the commandments: 'Do not commit adultery,' 'Do not murder,' 'Do not steal,' 'Do not bear false witness,' 'Do not defraud,' 'Honor your father and your mother.'"

And he answered and said to Him, "Teacher, all these things I have kept from my youth."

Then Jesus, looking at him, loved him, and said to him, "One thing you lack: Go your way, sell whatever you have and give to the poor, and you will have treasure in heaven; and come, take up the cross, and follow Me."

But he was sad at this word, and went away sorrowful, for he had great possessions.

To follow Jesus and to fulfill our calling, it will cost us something, in truth it will cost us everything. We need to be willing to let go of anything, before God entrusts us with the true wealth of His kingdom.

DELIVERANCE FROM THE SPIRIT OF POVERTY

Once you have learnt and understood the message of this book, it is time for you to take appropriate action.

Loose Each Area of Your Life

You need to loosen each area of your life that has been bound by this demon of poverty.

You must be determined to walk in God's love before you pray for your deliverance.

You can pray for self-deliverance over every aspect of your life where you experience lack, shortages, unproductivity, dissatisfaction, or unfulfillment.

When you pray, however, please don't pray a "bless me' prayer. You need to apply both *authority* and *power*. This means, with all your being, you must command! Imagine in your mind that you are running toward the enemy troops in battle, fully confident that you are going to win. This should be the attitude you exhibit in spiritual warfare for deliverance.

I need to remind you of some areas that are usually influenced by this demon of poverty:

- Marriage

- Health

- Finances

- Relationships

- Work

- Purpose

- Destiny

- Attitude

- Energy

- Love

- Victory

- Anointing

- Creativity

- Wisdom and knowledge

- Favor

- Generations

- Children

- Land

- Church

- Friendship

- Harvest

- Growth

- Body, and

Any other area the Holy Spirit brings to your remembrance.

This is not a one-time activity. You need to resist the devil at every moment and every time you encounter him daily.

A sample prayer

In the Name of Jesus Christ,

> I loose my marriage from the spirit of poverty by the authority that is vested upon me by my Lord. I command the fullness of God to manifest in my marriage. Let my marriage be on earth as it is in heaven.

> Let our communication, acceptance, attraction, and love be as God intended for these to be.

> I break the power of lack, of shortage, of impoverishment, and of dissatisfaction in the Name of Jesus Christ!

> I declare that we shall fulfill the purpose of God concerning our lives.

> Amen.

Test of Love

In the same manner that you do a regular medical check-up, you can do a love check-up by following the instructions below. This will show you whether you are living a healthy life in the area of love.

When you read the following verses taken from the love chapter of 1 Corinthians 13:4-8, write your name in the beginning of each verse below, instead of the word *love*:

_____ suffers long *and* is kind; _____ does not envy; _____ does not parade itself, is not puffed up; does not behave rudely, does not seek its own, is not provoked, thinks no evil; does not rejoice in iniquity, but rejoices in the truth; _____ bears all things, believes all things, hopes all things, endures all things.

WHERE DO WE GO FROM HERE?

After reading this, you may feel convicted by all the places and times you missed God in your walk with Him. Do not feel condemned. The purpose of this book is not to make anyone feel guilty or hopeless.

All the saints I mentioned in this book made their fair share of mistakes in their lives. In the religious world, we hear when a believer or a minister makes a mistake or falls, then they are no longer qualified to minister or preach again. However, were this the case, then we would need to remove the majority of the people whom God used—both from the Bible and whom we preached about.

Yes. Adam fell; Noah got drunk; Abraham lied and slept with his maid; Moses murdered a person; Joseph was accused of fornication and was incarcerated; Jacob was a deceiver; Isaac was a glutton; David committed adultery, killed his servant and stole his wife.

So too, Ruth was an outcast; Esther was an orphan; Jesus was born out of wedlock; Peter was impulsive, and denied Christ thrice; and Paul was chief among sinners.

For some reason, in today's religious world, when we hear about the mistakes of a fellow believer, we don't have the heart and mind to bear them up or to help restore them. We feel we are holier than them. This happens because of self-righteousness.

None of us are qualified to stand before a Holy God, or be used by Him. We are what we are because of His grace and mercy.

Do not let the enemy come with guilt and condemnation. Whatever happened in your life, whether children born out of wedlock, divorce, race, or whatever—nothing should stop you from fulfilling your kingdom assignment.

Why? A righteous person falls seven times, but he or she gets up and continues the journey. Do not listen to the religious spirit or your accusers.

We are supposed to forgive each other seventy-times-seven times a day.

Please keep the following verses in your heart, as you move forward with your calling:

> Who are you to judge another's servant? To his own master he stands or falls. Indeed, he will be made to stand, for God is able to make him stand. Romans 14:4

> Brethren, if a man is overtaken in any trespass, you who are spiritual restore such a one in a spirit of gentleness, considering yourself lest you also be tempted. Galatians 6:1

God Bless You!

G126 MOVEMENT

Children are our future and the future of a nation. If we don't reach them with the gospel of the kingdom, then there is no hope for us.

If you like to help poor and needy children, here's an opportunity we wish to present you. We are reaching thousands of children all over the world through our *Genesis 126 Movement*.

The harvest is plentiful, however trained and skilled laborers are few. We need both printed materials and laborers that are trained to use these, to go to schools and present the gospel of the kingdom to these young ones.

We have the opportunity, but we are looking for partners who will share this burden and extend and expend their resources towards a movement that is making a huge impact in the lives of these children.

If you like to know more about this, or would like to sponsor any aspect of this movement, please let us know. We can't do this alone. Together we can make a difference.

Please join us and either sponsor a child or sponsor a Trainer. Would you like to make a difference in one of these lives?

To know more about this visit
www.Treeof-Life.com

All gifts and donations made to Tree of Life are
tax-exempt in the USA.

More Books & Resources

DISCIPLING NATIONS SERIES

Kingdom Mandate (for any donation)
Discovering the Lost Kingdom (Volume 1) $14.00
Purpose, Calling, and Gifts (Volume 2) $15.00
God's Original Design (Volume 3) $20.00
Seeing, Entering, and Manifesting the Kingdom of God (Volume 4)$20.00
The Ekklesia (Volume 5) $30.00
The Gospel of the Kingdom (Volume 6) $20.00
Power and Authority of the Church (Volume 7) $15.00
Kingdom Family (Volume 8) $15.00
The Birthing of a Kingdom Nation (Volume 9) $20.00
What Happened to God? (Volume 10) $20.00
7 Dimensions and Operations of the Kingdom of God (Volume 11) $15.00
Kingdom Economy (Volume 12) $15.00
Kingdom Government (Volume 13) $15.00
Releasing Kings and Queens into God's Original Intent (Volume 14) $10.00
Kingdom Secrets to Restoring Nations Back to God (Volume 15) $20.00
Keys to Fulfilling Your Kingdom Assignment (Volume 16) $20.00

KINGDOM LIVING SERIES

The Three Most Important Decisions of Your Life $15.00
Recognizing God's Timing for Your Life $12.00
Overcoming the Spirit of Poverty $10.00
Seven Kinds of Believers $10.00
7 Dimensions of God's Glory $5.00
7 Dimensions of God's Grace $10.00
7 Kinds of Faith $8.00

HEALING OF THE NATIONS SERIES

Principles of Self Governance $20.00

KINGDOM BOOKS FOR KIDS

Genesis 126 Three Volume Book set for boys $25.00
Genesis 126 Three Volume Book set for boys $25.00

Genesis 126 Coloring Books for Boys $15.00
Genesis 126 Coloring Books for Girls $15.00

GENESIS 126 TEACHER'S MANUAL

Level 1 6-8 years $15.00
Level 2 8-10 years $15.00
Level 3 10-12 years $15.00

TO PLACE AN ORDER:

www.TheKingdomNetwork.org
Phone: 1-800-558-5020
Email: info@TheKingdomNetwork.org

www.ingramcontent.com/pod-product-compliance
Lightning Source LLC
Chambersburg PA
CBHW071556210326
41597CB00019B/3273